Quick Guide

MASONRY WALLS

CRE**A**TIVE
HOMEOWNER®

Editorial Director: David Schiff
Art Director: Annie Jeon

Author: Christine Beall, A.I.A.
Editor: Alexander Samuelson
Editorial Assistant: Georgette Blau
Copy Editor: Candice Levy, Ph.D.

Graphic Designer: Melisa DelSordo
Illustrators: Ron Carboni, Craig Franklin
Cover Design: Warren Ramezzana
Cover Illustrations: Craig Franklin

Current Printing (last digit)
10 9 8 7 6 5 4 3

Quick Guide: Masonry Walls
Library of Congress Catalog Card Number: 97-66870
ISBN: 1-880029-92-8

CREATIVE HOMEOWNER®
A Division of Federal Marketing Corp.
24 Park Way
Upper Saddle River, NJ 07458
Web site: **www.creativehomeowner.com**

C O N T E N T S

SAFETY FIRST

Though all the designs and methods in this book have been reviewed for safety, it is not possible to overstate the importance of using the safest construction methods possible. What follows are reminders; some do's and don'ts of basic carpentry. They are not substitutes for your own common sense.

- *Always* use caution, care, and good judgment when following the procedures described in this book.

- *Always* be sure that the electrical setup is safe; be sure that no circuit is overloaded and that all power tools and electrical outlets are properly grounded. Do not use power tools in wet locations.

- *Always* read container labels on paints, solvents, and other products; provide ventilation, and observe all other warnings.

- *Always* read the manufacturer's instructions for using a tool, especially the warnings.

- *Always* use hold-downs and push sticks whenever possible when working on a table saw. Avoid working short pieces if you can.

- *Always* remove the key from any drill chuck (portable or press) before starting the drill.

- *Always* pay deliberate attention to how a tool works so that you can avoid being injured.

- *Always* know the limitations of your tools. Do not try to force them to do what they were not designed to do.

- *Always* make sure that any adjustment is locked before proceeding. For example, always check the rip fence on a table saw or the bevel adjustment on a portable saw before starting to work.

- *Always* clamp small pieces firmly to a bench or other work surface when using a power tool on them.

- *Always* wear the appropriate rubber or work gloves when handling chemicals, moving or stacking lumber, or doing heavy construction.

- *Always* wear a disposable face mask when you create dust by sawing or sanding. Use a special filtering respirator when working with toxic substances and solvents.

- *Always* wear eye protection, especially when using power tools or striking metal on metal or concrete; a chip can fly off, for example, when chiseling concrete.

- *Always* be aware that there is seldom enough time for your body's reflexes to save you from injury from a power tool in a dangerous situation; everything happens too fast. Be *alert!*

- *Always* keep your hands away from the business ends of blades, cutters, and bits.

- *Always* hold a circular saw firmly, usually with both hands so that you know where they are.

- *Always* use a drill with an auxiliary handle to control the torque when large-size bits are used.

- *Always* check your local building codes when planning new construction. The codes are intended to protect public safety and should be observed to the letter.

- *Never* work with power tools when you are tired or under the influence of alcohol or drugs.

- *Never* cut tiny pieces of wood or pipe using a power saw. Cut small pieces off larger pieces.

- *Never* change a saw blade or a drill or router bit unless the power cord is unplugged. Do not depend on the switch being off; you might accidentally hit it.

- *Never* work in insufficient lighting.

- *Never* work while wearing loose clothing, hanging hair, open cuffs, or jewelry.

- *Never* work with dull tools. Have them sharpened, or learn how to sharpen them yourself.

- *Never* use a power tool on a workpiece—large or small—that is not firmly supported.

- *Never* saw a workpiece that spans a large distance between horses without close support on each side of the cut; the piece can bend, closing on and jamming the blade, causing saw kickback.

- *Never* support a workpiece from underneath with your leg or other part of your body when sawing.

- *Never* carry sharp or pointed tools, such as utility knives, awls, or chisels, in your pocket. If you want to carry such tools, use a special-purpose tool belt with leather pockets and holders.

TOOLS FOR MASONRY WORK

Building masonry walls is simple, hard work that requires a collection of simple, durable hand tools. You'll only need power tools if your wall requires a concrete footing. You'll need a circular saw to cut lumber for the footing, and you might want to rent a power mixer if you will be mixing the footing concrete yourself. This chapter describes the tools you'll need.

Tools of the Masonry Trade

You'll find that many of the same masonry tools are needed for working with concrete, brick, and stone. Many hand tools are available in a range of quality and corresponding price. When you buy, consider how often you will use the tool–no sense buying a top-notch trowel you'll use only once or twice.

Tools for Concrete Footings

Most masonry walls require a footing that extends below the frost line in your area. The footing prevents the wall from heaving and cracking when the moisture in the ground freezes. Dry-laid stone walls don't need footings because they can absorb ground movement.

Footings must, of course, be dug, so you'll need a spade and a flat shovel. If your footing is deep and large, you may want to rent a small front-end loader to excavate large sites, but be careful when using heavy machinery. It may be better to hire a contractor to do this work. Any kind of masonry work will require a wheelbarrow. Masonry loads are heavy, so be sure to buy or rent a heavy-duty wheelbarrow–one with a large capacity and an inflatable rubber tire.

For mixing and placing concrete, you'll need a mason's hoe. This tool is just like a gardener's hoe except there are two holes in the blade which help in the mixing of masonry materials. If you will be mixing your own concrete for the footing consider renting a power mixer. These are available in gasoline powered and electric powered models.

Measuring, Leveling, & Formwork Tools

All construction is an exercise in precision. It is essential that a project be correctly located, measured, leveled, and plumbed. Tools that assist in measuring masonry projects are a 48-inch level, a line level for

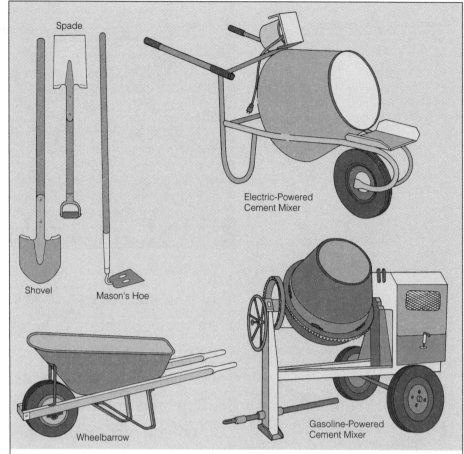

Tools for Concrete Footings. You'll need a spade and a flat shovel to dig footings. Use a wheelbarrow for transporting concrete and a mason's hoe for mixing it. Power mixers make the job easier.

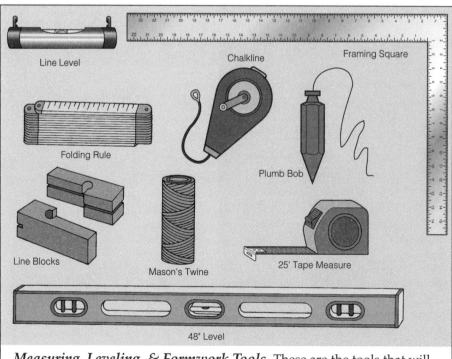

Measuring, Leveling, & Formwork Tools. These are the tools that will help you create masonry that is level, plumb, and straight.

long spans, a folding rule for brick projects, and a 25-foot tape measure. A framing square is needed to check for square in corners. Layout lines are marked with a chalkline. A plumb bob is used for checking that something is plumb or for marking a point directly under another point. Once marked, mason's twine is strung as a guide line to help you keep a structure straight, level, and plumb. Line blocks are used to keep the twine in place.

Tools for Working with Brick & Block

There are a number of specialized tools needed to work with mortar and bricks. A mortar box and mason's hoe are used for mixing and holding the mortar that binds the bricks together. A hawk (or mortar board) is a flat wood or metal foot-square surface that holds a bit of mortar when laying bricks. A hawk decreases trips to the mortar pile when you're working on a project. A brick hammer is helpful, as it has a curved point that can chip and split bricks. A brickset is a hardened-steel tool that easily splits and cuts bricks. You need a mason's trowel for spreading mortar. Jointing tools (jointers) are simply metal rods attached to a handle that are shaped to create various mortar joints. Examples are a round jointer or a square jointer. Be sure to have a mason's brush to clean excess mortar off a surface. A mason's brush is just like a dust brush. Brick-carrying tongs are large clamps that hold from 6 to 10 bricks. After a few loads, you'll be glad you bought one of these. You will also need a story pole to measure the correct height for vertical courses. You can make a story pole with a piece of scrap lumber marked in increments equal to the masonry units you're working with. For example, a story pole for standard brick construction is marked every 8 inches to delineate three courses of bricks plus their mortar joints.

Tools for Working with Stone

For stonework, you will need a brick hammer, which has a long curved point for splitting and shaping stones. A small sledge hammer (sometimes called a hand-drilling hammer) is heavy and is made of steel specifically designed for hitting other metal tools. A point chisel and a pitching chisel shape stone. Both chisels are made of steel that will not chip when struck with a hammer. A

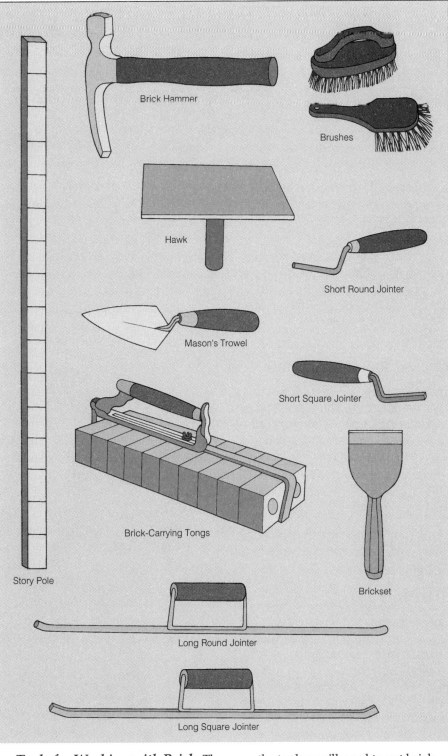

Brick Hammer

Brushes

Hawk

Short Round Jointer

Mason's Trowel

Short Square Jointer

Brick-Carrying Tongs

Story Pole

Brickset

Long Round Jointer

Long Square Jointer

Tools for Working with Brick. These are the tools you'll need to cut brick, build a brick wall that is straight and level, and create neat mortar joints.

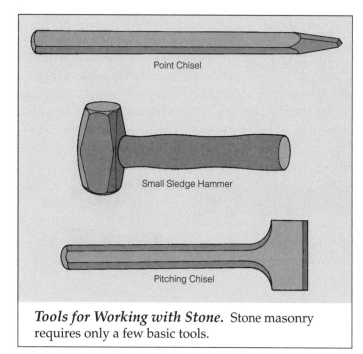

Tools for Working with Stone. Stone masonry requires only a few basic tools.

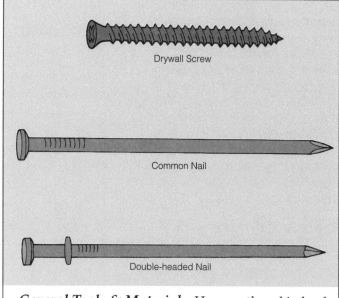

General Tools & Materials. Here are three kinds of fasteners commonly used in masonry work.

point chisel is slender and is used for precise chipping; a pitching chisel is broad to split stones. If the stone structure is held with mortar, you'll need the mortar tools used for brick construction.

General Tools & Materials

These are tools you probably already own. To help in masonry construction and to build formwork you need a claw hammer and a circular saw. You can use a crosscut saw if you don't own a circular saw. Formwork is held together by either double-headed nails (also called duplex nails), 2-inch drywall screws, or galvanized common nails. You'll also need a heavy-duty extension cord and carpenter's pencils.

Masonry Safety

Concrete and mortar are caustic and will burn the skin after prolonged contact. Wear sturdy work gloves and clothing with long sleeves to protect your hands and arms when working with mortar. Wear rubber boots when placing and handling concrete because you may have to stand in the wet mix to spread the fresh concrete. To protect your eyes from cement dust and from splattered mortar or concrete, wear safety glasses or goggles. Since masonry involves heavy lifting, be careful to avoid back strain and injury. Always bend your knees, keep your back straight, and lift with your legs.

Masonry Safety. Masonry work invariably involves some heavy lifting. Lift with your legs, not your back.

BUILDING CONCRETE FOOTINGS

A proper footing is essential to the long life of any mortared masonry wall. The footing provides a stable, unmoving base that protects your wall from being destroyed by ground movement. In this chapter you will learn to build the wooden formwork for a footing and mix and pour the concrete to fill the form.

Concrete Footings

Concrete footings are used to support garden walls of brick, block, or mortared stone. Footings are set below the local frost line depth to avoid damage from frost heave. The depth to which the soil freezes depends not only on climate and geographic location but also on soil composition, altitude, and weather patterns. In North America, particularly in western and northern locales, patterns of freezing can vary widely within a small area. It is imperative that you consult your local building department to determine frost line depth and how much farther a footing should reach below that line.

Planning the Footing

Building codes are very specific about footing requirements for various structures, so get information from your local building department before starting any work. In areas with extremely deep frost lines, it may not be practical to dig the wall footing below the frost line; you could end up with more wall beneath the ground than above it. In such cases, the footing sits on at least 8 inches of compacted, well-drained gravel that

is laid above the frost line. If at all possible, however, it's always best to set footings below the frost line, where freezing and thawing soil won't push the wall up and down. In soil with poor drainage (regardless of frost line depth), place the footing on a tamped gravel base at least 6 inches thick. The gravel base prevents water from accumulating beneath the footing, keeping soil movement to a minimum. If you are unsure of the soil type, ask your local building officials about the types of wall footings they recommend. Footings for walls must be sturdy and strong to support the weight they will carry.

The footing depth should be the same as the wall thickness, or a minimum of 8 inches. The footing width should be twice the wall thickness, or a minimum of 16 inches.

Wooden forms are used for shaping a footing. If you can dig a trench without the sidewalls crumbling, then the earth itself can be used as forms. In most cases, however, form boards are required to make accurate, level footings. Use wide boards (2x6s, 2x8s, 2x10s, etc.) that extend to the full depth of the footing, or, if the soil will hold a vertical edge, dig the rim of the trench wider to accommodate

narrow boards, such as 2x4s, that will serve as guides for leveling the top of the concrete footing.

Poured concrete can exert considerable pressure on the forms, so they should be held in position with 1x4 stakes driven into the ground and nailed to the forms every few feet and 1x4 spreaders nailed every few feet along the top of the form boards. Use double-headed nails so that you can dismantle the forms easily after the concrete has set.

Locating & Excavating

Once you've established where to build a wall, use stakes, string, and batter boards to mark the footing location and to guide you in excavating trenches and setting up any forms. You can use the following instructions for either a freestanding straight wall or for one with corners. If your wall will define property lines, be sure the footing is properly positioned according to easement regulations.

1 **Locating the Wall Ends and Corners.** Drive stakes in the ground to represent both 90-degree corners of the wall or, for straight freestanding walls, the outer corners of the wall at each end.

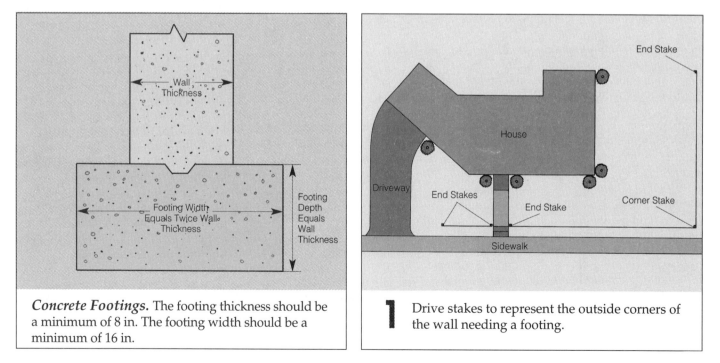

Concrete Footings. The footing thickness should be a minimum of 8 in. The footing width should be a minimum of 16 in.

1 Drive stakes to represent the outside corners of the wall needing a footing.

2 Erecting the Batter Boards.

Measure out 3 to 4 feet beyond each stake, and erect a set of batter boards, as shown. The batter board crosspieces (the horizontal members) should be at least 1 foot wider than the anticipated width of the footing trench, with the center roughly aligned to the center point of the proposed wall.

Using the stakes as guides, attach a string to the batter boards to represent the outside face of the wall. At the corners, use the 3-4-5 triangulation method to make sure the strings meet at 90 degrees. To do this simply remember that if one side of a right triangle measures 3 feet, and the other measures 4 feet, then the hypotenuse must measure 5 feet. If any of these measurements is off, then the corner is not square.

3 Setting the Strings and Excavating.

On the batter board crosspieces, measure the wall width from the string and mark the other face of the wall (labeled A in the illustration); the inside and outside faces of the footing (B); and the outside edges of the footing trench (C). The footing width is either twice as wide as the wall or two-thirds the wall height, whichever is greater. The trench should be 1 or 2 feet wider than the footing to provide room for installing the formwork. At each mark, drive a nail to tie the string to the board.

When the strings are set and squared, mark with sand below lines C to delineate the excavation for the trench. Then excavate to the depth of the footing and the required gravel base.

Building the Formwork

Before building the forms, add a gravel base, if needed. Add half the amount and tamp to level. Then add the rest of the gravel to provide adequate drainage. You must consult your local building department about the depth of the required gravel base.

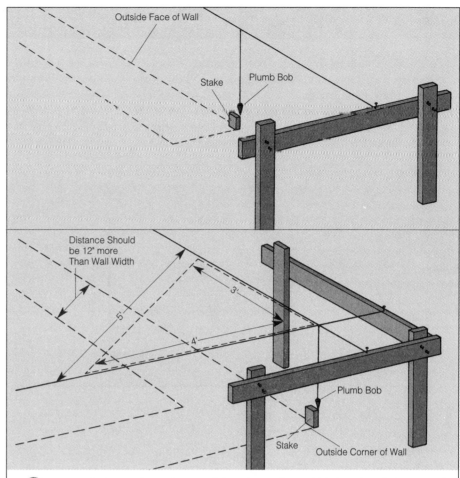

2 A single batter board is used for a straight wall (above), while two boards are placed at a right angle to mark corners (below).

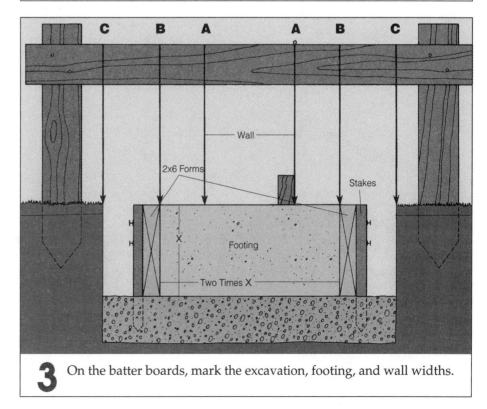

3 On the batter boards, mark the excavation, footing, and wall widths.

For footings in firm, dry soil, wooden forms can be eliminated and the concrete can be formed by the earth trench. Excavate a trench that is the exact width of the footing, using a spade to keep the edges straight. Make the trench deep enough so that the top of the footing will be about 2 to 3 inches below finished grade and

drive a row of wooden stakes down the middle to indicate the top of the concrete. Use a straight 2x4 and a level to make sure the tops of the guide stakes are level. When the concrete is poured, simply smooth the surface with a float so that it is even with the tops of the stakes.

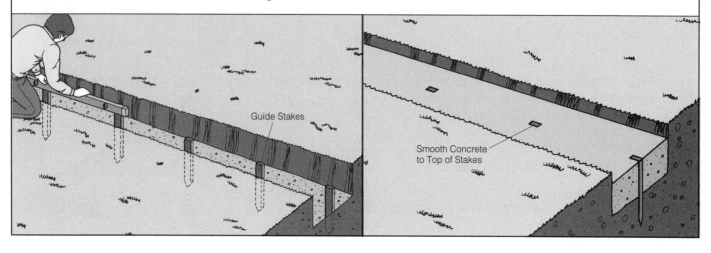

Guide Stakes

Smooth Concrete to Top of Stakes

1 Locating the Footing Corners. First, reattach the strings representing the edges of the footing (B strings) to the batter boards. At the ends of the footing, or where corner strings intersect, hang a plumb bob to the bottom of the trench. At these points, drive short lengths of rebar into the ground. Drive them deep below the proposed footing surface. These rebar stakes represent the ends of a straight

footing or the inside and outside corners of an L-shaped footing.

2 Installing the Corner Stakes. Hold a small piece of the form material against the rebar at the outside corners and drive two 1x4 stakes a few inches from the rebar. These stakes will support the corners of the outside form boards. The tops of the stakes should be level with each other and equal to the top of the form boards. If you're placing an

L-shaped footing (a corner), you can, for now, ignore the rebar driven at inside corners.

3 Installing the Intermediate Stakes. Stretch leveled strings between the corner stakes, and use the strings as guides to install intermediate stakes about every 4 feet to support the form boards. If the form boards are long enough to reach between the corner stakes, you may find it easier to attach and

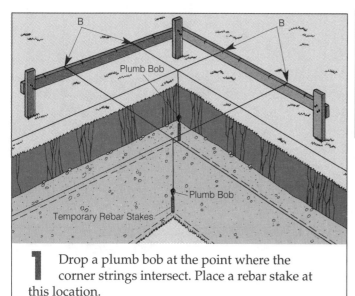

B   B

Plumb Bob

Plumb Bob

Temporary Rebar Stakes

1 Drop a plumb bob at the point where the corner strings intersect. Place a rebar stake at this location.

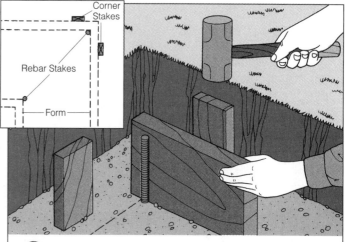

Corner Stakes

Rebar Stakes

Form

2 Place a corner stake away from the rebar stakes at a distance equal to the thickness of the form board.

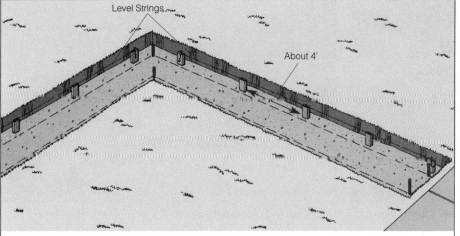

Level Strings

About 4'

3 Stretch leveled strings between the corner stakes and use the strings as guides to install intermediate stakes every 4 ft. to support the form boards.

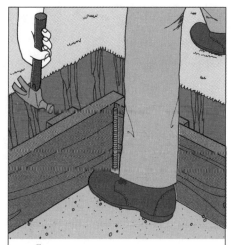

4 Attach the form boards to the stakes with double-headed nails.

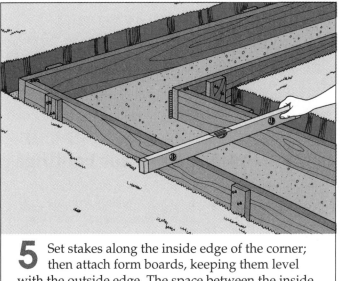

5 Set stakes along the inside edge of the corner; then attach form boards, keeping them level with the outside edge. The space between the inside and outside edge equals the footing width.

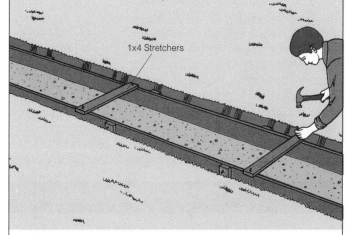

1x4 Stretchers

6 Install 1x4 stretchers across the board tops at 4- to 6-ft. intervals to keep the concrete from spreading the forms. Deep forms may require additional bracing.

level the form boards first, then use them as a guide to install the intermediate stakes.

4 Installing the Form Boards. Attach the form boards by driving nails or screws through the stakes into the boards. While nailing, place your foot against the inside of the board to keep from knocking the stake out of position. As long as the stakes are level, you can align the top edges of the boards with the tops of the stakes. Check the form boards frequently with a 4-foot level to make sure they remain even.

5 Setting Up the Inside Forms. Use the outside form boards to locate the stakes for the inside forms. Beginning a few inches from the inside corner rebar, drive stakes every 4 feet or so. Locate the stakes so that when you attach the form boards, the space between the forms equals the footing width. Set the stakes along one edge of the footing first, making sure they are level. Then, at the inside corner, align a form board with the rebar and attach the board to the stakes. Every few feet, lay a level across the inside and outside form boards, as shown, to be sure they are level with each other.

Set the stakes for the adjacent inside form, then attach a form board. Butt the end of this board against the one that is already in place and toenail the top edge to keep the boards flush. Check for level and perfect square.

6 Bracing the Formwork. If the form boards are 2x6s or wider, install 1x4 stretchers across the board tops at 4- to 6-foot intervals to keep the concrete from spreading the forms. Deep forms that are built with multiple boards may require extra bracing.

Adding Reinforcement. Rebar is laid in the footing form. Follow local building codes for proper reinforcement of footings.

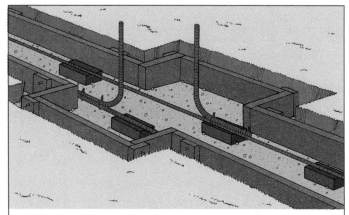

Pilasters. Install short sections of rebar turned up. The vertical leg should be at least 18 in. high. The horizontal leg should be at least 12 in. long.

Adding Reinforcement

Place horizontal rebar in the footing trench, according to local building codes. Footings require rebar and not reinforcing mesh or ready-mix infused with fibers. For shallow footings, use bricks to prop the rebar above the trench bottom; rebar should be about one-third the way up from the bottom of the footing. For deeper footings, you can tie the horizontal rebar to short vertical rebars driven into the ground. Keep the bars at least 1 inch away from the form boards or trench sides.

Where two pieces of reinforcing bar must be spliced together, lap them 30 times the diameter of the bar, or a minimum of 12 inches, and tie them securely together with twisted wire. For example, if the bar is ½ inch diameter, the overlap should be 15 inches (30x½). Intersecting reinforcing bars should also be tied to hold them together when the concrete is poured.

Pilasters. If your footing is for a masonry wall with pilasters, install short sections of rebar that will turn up into the masonry. The vertical leg should be at least 18 inches high, and the horizontal leg at least 12 inches long.

Concrete for Footings

There are two ways to obtain concrete for your footing. You can buy the ingredients and mix them yourself, or your can order the concrete ready-mixed and delivered by truck.

If you order by truck, you simply need to know how much concrete you need. The supplier will know the best mixture to use for a footing in your area.

Concrete Ingredients

If you are mixing your own concrete you need to use the proper ingredients in the proper proportions. Fresh concrete is a semifluid mixture of portland cement, sand (fine aggregate), gravel or crushed stone (coarse aggregate), and water. As the cement particles chemically react with water, in a process called *hydration,* the concrete hardens into a durable material.

Portland Cement. There are five types of portland cement, each

Stepped Footing Forms

Where the ground under a wall slopes slightly, you can build a level footing that is deeper in the ground at one end than the other. Where the ground slopes steeply, it is best to step the form down the slope so that the footing is in a series of level sections. For footings without forms, step the excavation down and form a dam with a board or piece of plywood and wooden stakes driven into the sides of the excavation. For footings with lumber forms, build two overlapping forms to create the change in height.

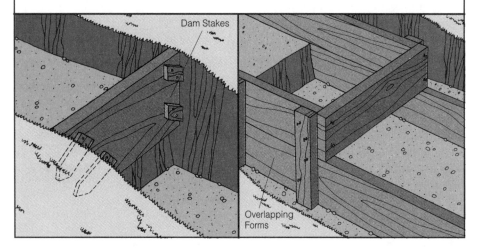

Dam Stakes

Overlapping Forms

with different physical and chemical characteristics.

■ Type I is a general-purpose cement that is by far the most commonly used, especially in residential work. This is the type of cement you should use, unless your project has special requirements that would benefit from the characteristics of one of the other types of portland cement.

■ Type II cement has moderate resistance to sulfates, which are found in some soils and ground water. If you're not sure about the soil in your area, ask your supplier if local builders typically use this cement.

■ Type III cement is a high-early-strength cement. This means that it gains strength more quickly than other types, not that it develops greater strength. A cement with a short curing time can be helpful for winter construction because fresh concrete must be protected from freezing. If you have to build during the cold winter months, consider Type III cement. (An extra bag of Type I in a concrete mix can produce similar results as using a Type III cement.)

■ Type IV cement produces less heat during hydration than other types and is used only in massive structures such as dams and highway pilings. It's not appropriate for residential construction.

■ Type V cement has a high resistance to sulfates. This type of cement is usually available only in areas where it is likely to be needed—for example, in the U.S. Southwest. Ask your supplier if local builders generallyuse Type V cement.

Most building centers sell portland cement. Each bag contains about 1 cubic foot of cement and weighs 94 pounds. Don't let the bags get wet during storage–the cement will react with water and harden, making them unusable. Bags of cement must be stored up off the ground; otherwise, they can absorb moisture. They also should not be stored on a concrete floor as they can absorb moisture through the concrete. Stack

them on wooden skids; then cover the bags with plastic.

Aggregates. Cement and water form the paste that binds together gravel or crushed stone (coarse aggregate) and sand (fine aggregate). Since these aggregates are much cheaper than cement, they act as an inexpensive filler to make concrete a practical and economical building material. Aggregates also help reduce shrinkage of concrete.

Coarse aggregate is sold by the cubic foot or cubic yard and can be purchased directly from an aggregate company. The mix should include particle sizes ranging from ¼ to 1 inch in diameter–the smaller aggregate particles fill in the spaces between the larger ones. Do not use aggregate that is larger than one-quarter of the concrete's thickness.

The sand particles used as fine aggregate in concrete must measure less than ¼ inch in diameter to fill in the spaces between the pieces of coarse aggregate. Concrete sand should not be the sharp type found in sand made from crushed rock. Instead use "bank-run" sand. The naturally rounded shape of bank-run sand makes the concrete easier to work with and slab surfaces easier to finish. Never use mason's sand or beach sand. You can purchase small

amounts of concrete sand at a home center; get larger amounts from an aggregate supplier.

Water. The final ingredient in concrete is water, which must be free of foreign materials and impurities. A rule of thumb is to use only water that is fit to drink.

Air-Entrained Cement

Type I, II, and III cements are available with an additive that produces evenly distributed microscopic air bubbles in the mix. When manufactured in this way, the cement is said to be "air-entrained," and the letter A is appended to the type number (e.g., Type IA). The air bubbles permit enough space for the water in the concrete to expand when frozen, keeping the concrete from cracking. Air-entrainment improves the durability of concrete that is exposed to freeze-thaw cycles and to de-icing salts. Be aware that hand mixing is ineffective for air-entrained concrete; you must use a power mixer. If you need air-entrained concrete, use either an air-entraining cement, or use regular cement with an air-entraining admixture.

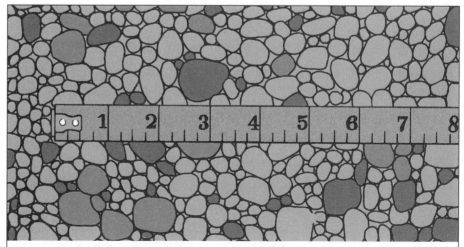

Aggregates. The aggregate in concrete ranges in size from ¼ to 1 in. in diameter. Do not use aggregate larger than one-quarter the thickness of the concrete.

Whether you mix your own or have your concrete delivered to the site, the amount of water used in a concrete mix affects the ultimate strength the concrete will develop. You want a consistency that makes the concrete easy to pour, move around in the forms, consolidate, and finish. Up to a point, a mix with more water is easier to work with than one having less water. But too much water will cause the ingredients to separate during pouring and handling, ruining the concrete. Too much water also lowers strength, increases the porosity and permeability of the cured concrete, and makes the concrete more prone to shrinkage and cracking. The trick is to use enough water to make the concrete workable, but not so much that it creates a weak or porous material. In most instances, professional masons use 4 to 5 gallons of water per bag of cement, depending on the dampness of the sand.

Calculating Concrete Amounts

Ready-mixed concrete is sold by the cubic yard. Because footings are rectangular, it's easy to calculate how much concrete you will need. Find the volume by multiplying the width in feet times the length in feet times the height in inches (WxLxH). Divide the final number by 12 to get cubic feet. The figure determined by this calculation is rounded up to the nearest whole number (e.g., 52.7 becomes 53). Then divide this number by 27 to convert to cubic yards. Add 10 percent extra to make sure you have enough.

Mixing Your Own Concrete

If you are mixing your own concrete you'll need to use the ingredients in the proper proportions. Use the table "Concrete Proportions by Volume" below to determine the proportions of cement, sand, gravel, and water required. For estimating purposes, you can make about 1 cubic yard of concrete with five 94-pound bags of cement, 14 cubic feet of sand, and 21 cubic feet of gravel. (It takes about forty 80-pound bags of prepackaged materials to make 1 cubic yard of concrete.)

Note that the volume of the combined ingredients is about one-third less than the sum of the volumes of the individual ingredients. For example, if you use 1 cubic foot of cement, 2¼ cubic feet of sand, 1½ cubic feet of gravel, or crushed stone, and ½ cubic foot of water, you get a combined total volume of 5¼ cubic feet. But the mix will actually produce 3½ cubic feet of concrete (or two-thirds of the combined total).

If you do not need this much concrete or you want to work with smaller batches, use the same proportions, but with smaller quantities, substituting buckets for cubic feet. (For the mix proportions given previously, you'd use 1 bucket of cement, 2¼ buckets of sand, 1½ buckets of gravel and ½ bucket of water.) For any batch size, the most important thing is to keep the proportions of the ingredients the same. You can double or triple the batch size simply by doubling or tripling the number of buckets of each ingredient you add to the mix.

Mixing Concrete On Site

If you need less than 1 cubic yard of concrete or if ready-mix delivery is not available, you can mix your own concrete on site either by hand or with a power mixer. When mixing concrete by any method, make sure to protect yourself by wearing long sleeves, long pants, and heavy waterproof gloves. If concrete accidentally spatters on your skin, wash it off immediately, as it causes burning irritation.

Mixing Concrete by Hand. If your project will be exposed to repeated freeze-thaw cycles, you cannot hand mix the concrete because you won't be able to stir vigorously enough to produce the proper air entrainment. Hand mixing concrete involves using a square-point shovel or a mason's hoe to combine the ingredients. Hand mixing is hard work. While you can mix the ingredients in a wheelbarrow, it's usually easier to mix them on a clean, flat surface, such as an old sheet of plywood, or in a mortar box (also called a concrete barge).

Testing Water Content. Note that the sand used to make the concrete should be wet, but not too wet. Proper sand will hold a ball shape without wetting your hand. Very wet sand will make a ball and "leak" water, while

Maximum Size Coarse Aggregate, Inches	Air-Entrained Concrete				Concrete without Air			
	Number of Parts per Ingredient				Number of Parts per Ingredient			
	Cement	Sand*	Coarse Aggregate	Water	Cement	Sand*	Coarse Aggregate	Water
⅜	1	2¼	1½	½	1	2½	1½	½
½	1	2¼	2	½	1	2½	2	½
¾	1	2¼	2½	½	1	2½	2½	½
1	1	2¼	2¾	½	1	2½	2¾	½
1½	1	2¼	3	½	1	2½	3	½

Note: 7.48 gallons of water equals 1 cubic foot. One 94-lb. bag of portland cement equals about 1 cubic foot.
* "wet" sand sold for most construction use.
The combined finished volume is approximately two-thirds the sum of the original bulk volumes.

dry sand crumbles and will not hold a shape. If the sand is too dry, wet it thoroughly with a garden hose the day before beginning work. Always cover your sand pile with a sheet of plastic when you're not working, to prevent the sand from drying out.

Here's how to mix concrete ingredients by hand:

1 Measuring the Ingredients. For mixing purposes, you can measure proportions by the bucket, by the shovelful, or with a measuring box, like the one shown in the illustration. A measuring box is built to hold exactly 1 cubic foot of dry ingredients, as opposed to a concrete barge, mortar box, or other container in which wet and dry ingredients are combined. Use the same amount of each ingredient for each batch. Careful measuring ensures correct proportions. Place the materials in layers on top of each other, beginning with the gravel, then the sand, and finally the cement.

2 Mixing the Dry Ingredients. If you're working on a flat surface or mixing the ingredients in a wheelbarrow, use a mason's hoe to combine the dry ingredients thoroughly before adding the water. When using a mortar box, you can either premix

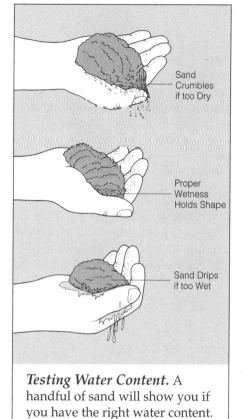

Testing Water Content. A handful of sand will show you if you have the right water content.

Sand Crumbles if too Dry

Proper Wetness Holds Shape

Sand Drips if too Wet

the dry ingredients or mix them together as you add the water.

3 Adding the Water. Start with a gallon of water and keep track of the amount you use so that you can add the same amount to subsequent batches. Make sure to mix

all ingredients thoroughly, scraping any unmixed cement and aggregate from the sides and bottom of the box or pile. The concrete mix should be an even color and have the same consistency throughout.

If you are mixing on a flat surface, make a shallow depression in the center of the dry mix with your hoe, then pour in a little water. Mix thoroughly by pulling dry material from the edges into the depression. If you are using a mortar box, place the dry materials so they fill about two-thirds of the box (from one end), leaving the rest of the box empty (on the side nearest the forms). Add water to the empty end, then pull the dry materials into the water, mixing them together as you go. Continue adding water in small amounts while turning over the mix until it reaches the proper consistency: not crumbly, not sloppy.

4 Testing the Mix. You can tell if the concrete has too little or too much water by using the blade of your hoe or shovel to make ridges in the concrete. If the mix is too dry, you won't be able to make distinct ridges; if the mix is too soupy, the ridges won't hold their shape (you'll also notice water seeping out around the edges of the pile). In a proper

1 A measuring box holds exactly 1 cu. ft. of dry ingredients. Use one to proportion the ingredients.

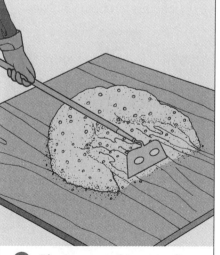

2 If you are working on a flat surface or mixing in a wheelbarrow, use a mason's hoe to mix the dry ingredients.

3 Make a depression in the middle of the dry ingredients. Add water slowly and pull the dry mix into the water.

4 In a proper mix, ridges made with a mason's hoe will hold their shape.

mix, the ridges will hold most of their shape. If the mix is too wet, it usually doesn't have enough sand and coarse aggregate for the amount of cement. Add a little more sand and aggregate, mix well and retest. Keep careful notes on the added amounts.

If the mix is too stiff, it has too much aggregate. Remedy the problem by adding a mixture of two parts cement to one part water. If this does not work, discard the batch, and make a new one, using less sand and gravel. Write down the proportions used so that you can make subsequent batches of the same consistency.

Using a Power Mixer. If you don't want to mix your concrete by hand, you can rent a small concrete mixer with a capacity ranging from ½ to 6 cubic feet. Electric mixers are quieter and simpler to operate than gasoline-powered mixers, but you must have access to an electrical outlet. If an extension cord is required, make sure the wire gauge is heavy enough to handle the ampere draw of the motor. The size of the concrete batch is usually only about 60 percent of the total capacity of the mixer to allow room for proper mixing without spilling. Never load a mixer beyond its maximum batch size.

As previously stated, be sure to use the correct proportions of concrete

ingredients. For best results, follow this procedure: With the mixer stopped, add all the coarse aggregate and half the water. Start the mixer, then add the sand, cement, and remaining water. After all ingredients are in the drum, continue mixing for at least three minutes or until the ingredients are thoroughly mixed and the concrete has a uniform color.

Thoroughly clean the mixer as soon as you have finished using it. Place water and a few shovelfuls of coarse aggregate into the drum while it is turning, to scour the inside of the mixer. Then dump out the water and gravel, and hose out the drum.

Handling & Pouring Concrete

First, check all formwork for proper grade and correct depth. Once you're sure that everything is in its proper place, spray the inside surfaces of the forms and the soil or gravel subgrade with water from a garden hose. This will keep them from drawing too much water from the concrete, which can create a poor quality surface or weakened concrete.

Be sure to wear rubber boots, protective clothing, and gloves, because prolonged contact with fresh concrete will burn your skin.

Mix your concrete as near the job site as you can or have the concrete truck park as close as possible. Use a wheelbarrow to move the concrete from the mixing area or from the truck to the project site. Lay 2x12s across lawn areas to protect them from the weight of the wheelbarrow.

Start dumping the concrete at the farthest end of the forms, making piles that are slightly taller than the forms. Be sure to fill the forms completely. Fill low areas with a shovel; spade the concrete to fill in corners. Settle the concrete against the perimeter forms by tapping the outside of the form boards with a hammer.

As soon as the first section of the form is filled, begin leveling, or screeding, the concrete. Use a straight length of 2x4 that is slightly wider than the form. Drag it along the top of the forms, pressing down firmly. Fill any hollow areas with a shovel and strike them off level. Since the concrete will not be exposed to view, no other finishing is required.

Removing the forms. After the concrete has cured for a day or two, carefully remove the forms. Do not pry or hammer against the concrete itself. The concrete will continue to cure slowly for another month until it reaches full strength, but it is strong enough to begin the wall construction after the first week.

Handling & Pouring Concrete. Start dumping the concrete at the farthest end of the forms. Fill the forms completely. Fill any low areas with a shovel; tamp the concrete to fill in corners.

WORKING WITH BRICK AND BLOCK

Brick has been used as a building material for several thousand years. Bricklaying is easy to learn, and even a first-timer can produce a pleasing finished product. The techniques are simple and methodical, and there's a sense of accomplishment that comes with the steady progress of a brick project.

Concrete block is a much newer material than brick, but it has become popular for its durability, versatility, and economy. This chapter covers the techniques of constructing garden walls and retaining walls from brick and concrete block.

Choosing Brick

Brick is made from clay that is molded to shape and fired at very high temperatures in a large kiln or oven. The color of the natural clay determines the color of the brick, although some manufacturers combine more than one clay to produce a variety of colored brick from off-white to almost black. Brick textures vary, depending on the molding process. Since brick distributors handle the products of several manufacturers, there should be a wide selection of materials available to you.

Brick made in the United States and Canada today is extremely dense, hard, and durable. If the units are shaped by extruding the clay through a die, they usually have holes through the middle. These holes make the bricks lighter in weight and more economical and increase the bricks' bond to the mortar. This type of brick is used for wall construction where the holes are not visible.

The best way to choose brick for your project is to visit a local brick distributor where you can look at sample panels or project photographs-- these will give you a good idea of what the finished masonry will look like. Colors and textures will vary from one manufacturer to another. A color that has a wide range of light and dark shades as well as "blends," which combine more than one color, will be more difficult to work with than a single color with relatively few shades. Light and dark units must be carefully mixed together as a project is built so that you don't accidentally create zigzag patterns or blotches of color.

Face Brick. Face brick is used when consistency in appearance is required. A batch of face brick will be quite uniform in color, size, texture, and face surface. Face brick comes in three types, differentiated by appearance. Type FBA (architectural) brick has no limits on size variations or on the amount of chips and cracks

that are permitted. This type includes hand-molded brick as well as extruded brick that is tumbled or rolled before firing to soften the edges or dent the surfaces. This is a popular type of brick for residential construction because the units resemble old brick. Type FBS (standard) brick is used in commercial applications more than on residences. The dimensions don't vary as much from one unit to the next, the edges are sharper, and there are fewer chips and cracks permitted. Type FBX (extra) brick has the tightest limits on size variation, chips, and cracks. The edges are very sharp, and the crisp outline gives these units a very contemporary look. This type is not as popular, even for commercial projects.

Bricks similar to those used in historic buildings are produced by some manufacturers. The units are formed and shaped by pressing the clay into a mold by hand or by machine, giving the brick a weathered and rustic look. These molded bricks are relatively porous and will absorb more water than extruded bricks. Many suppliers will also stock actual used brick. Molded bricks do not have core holes in the center but may have an indentation called a "frog." Used brick has a charming irregular quality and is structurally sound, but unpredictable durability makes it risky for exterior use.

Building Brick. Building bricks, or common bricks as they are sometimes called, are rough in appearance but structurally sound. The chips, cracks, and slight deformations in building brick create a rustic look and these units are less expensive than face brick.

Paving Brick and Firebrick. Paving brick is always solid, because in paving, the widest faces are visible. Paving brick is classified by its appearance in the same way as face brick: PA (architectural), PS (standard), and PX (extra). Firebrick is made of a special clay and is baked at an extremely high temperature to make the units resistant to high heat. Firebrick is used to line fireplaces, ovens, and furnaces. You won't need paving brick or firebrick for projects in this book.

Sizes & Shapes of Brick

Building and face brick come in many different sizes, but the easiest size to work with is called modular brick. The basic unit is 3⅝ inches wide, 2¼ inches thick, and 7⅝ inches long. The measured dimensions of the units themselves are called the actual dimensions; the dimensions of a unit plus one mortar joint are called the nominal dimensions. When laid with standard ⅜-inch mortar joints, the nominal length is rounded up to 8 inches. Three bricks laid with the large bed surface one on top of the other and with ⅜-inch mortar joints between measure 8 inches high. By rounding up to include

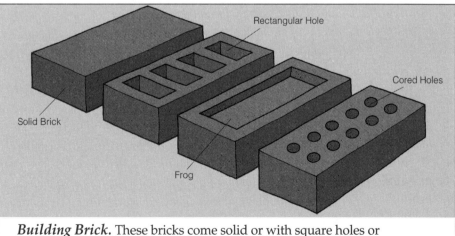

Building Brick. These bricks come solid or with square holes or indentations called frogs. Some have a series of round "cored" holes.

mortar joints, you can easily plan wall lengths and opening locations and minimize brick cutting. Rounding up also makes it easy to combine brick with other types of modular masonry units, such as concrete block.

Special Shapes. Some brick manufacturers make special shapes such as wall copings, angled corner brick, and radial units for curved walls. Specially shaped units cost more, but they can add a distinctive touch to your designs.

Calculating How Many Bricks You Need

Laying out brick units is simple when you set the length and width of walls, patios, or walks to a multiple of 4 inches. With nominal 8-inch brick, use a 4-inch module because that is the length of half a brick. The importance of brick halves is that they create a staggered layout in the bond pattern. For example, make a brick wall 80 inches long (a multiple of 4 inches) rather than 78 inches long. Likewise, make a brick sidewalk 36 inches wide rather than 30 inches because 36 is a multiple of 4. Any openings that are planned should also be located and sized on the 4-inch module. This will mean that only whole and half-size units will be needed, and a minimum number of units will have to be cut.

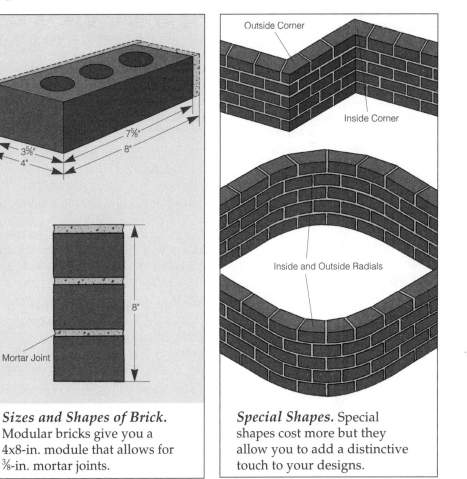

Sizes and Shapes of Brick. Modular bricks give you a 4x8-in. module that allows for ⅜-in. mortar joints.

Special Shapes. Special shapes cost more but they allow you to add a distinctive touch to your designs.

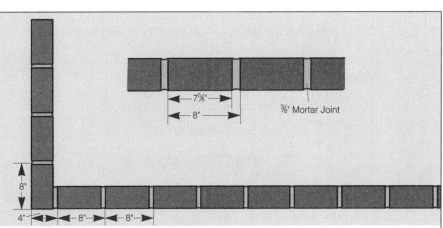

Calculating How Many Bricks You Need. Whenever possible, plan brick wall lengths in multiples of 4 in. to allow you to use only full and half bricks.

For estimating purposes, figure about seven bricks (nominally 4 by 8 inches) for every square foot of area in a wall. Area is determined by the length times the height of a wall. Remember to double the estimate for a wall that is two brick widths (called wythes) thick. A wythe is a vertical section of a wall that is equal to the width of the masonry unit. Typical garden walls are two wythes wide. Estimate about four and a half bricks for every square foot when paving bricks are laid broad face, horizontally on the ground.

Water Absorption. Some brick is very dry and will absorb a lot of water from the mortar. This causes a poor bond between the brick and mortar. To test a brick for excessive absorption, draw a circle the size of a quarter on the bed surface of the brick using a crayon or wax pencil. With a medicine dropper, place 12 drops of water inside the circle; time how long it takes for the water to be absorbed. If the water is absorbed in less than one minute, the brick is too dry. Thoroughly wet the bricks with a garden hose the day before you will lay them. Let them dry for an entire 24-hour period.

Concrete Block

One of the most economical masonry materials is concrete block. These masonry units consist of an outside shell with a hollow center that is divided by two or three vertical webs.

Water Absorption. If it takes less than one minute for the brick to absorb 12 drops of water, the brick is too dry.

The ends of a unit may have flanges that accept mortar and join with the adjacent block, or they may have smooth ends for corners and the end of walls. Concrete block is manufactured throughout the United States and the exact design, texture, and color may differ slightly from area to area.

Although called concrete, these blocks are not the same as the concrete used for footings and other poured concrete projects. The blocks are composed of different materials including cement, sand, and a variety of very small aggregates such as gravel and cinders. There are various types of blocks, such as solid, load-bearing, and non-load-bearing. The heavy blocks made with sand and gravel or crushed stone can weigh more than 50 pounds each; working with them can be

back breaking if you're not accustomed to heavy lifting. Lighter units made with coal cinders, slag, and other aggregates may weigh as little as 22 pounds, but they are less resistant to moisture absorption. Be sure to ask your supplier about what type of block to use for your project.

Concrete block construction is as prone to shrinkage cracking as are concrete slabs and sidewalks. The shrinkage cracking in concrete masonry construction is controlled in the same way as they are in concrete slabs—with steel reinforcement and control joints. Approximately every 20 feet along a wall's length, a control joint takes the place of a vertical mortar joint to regulate cracking.

Concrete Block Characteristics

Standard concrete blocks have an actual face size of 7⅝ inches by 15 ⅝ inches. When you add the thickness of a standard ⅜-inch mortar joint, the block measures 8 by 16 inches—its nominal size. The most commonly used block thickness is also nominally 8 inches (7⅝ inches actual dimension), but you can get nominal 4-, 6-, 10-, and 12-inch thicknesses, too. Three modular bricks including their mortar joints are the same height as one modular 8-inch concrete block; two modular brick lengths equal one modular block length.

Stretcher Core Styles. A basic concrete block unit is called a

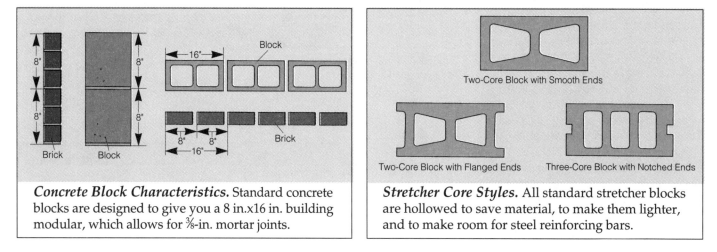

Concrete Block Characteristics. Standard concrete blocks are designed to give you a 8 in.x16 in. building modular, which allows for ⅜-in. mortar joints.

Stretcher Core Styles. All standard stretcher blocks are hollowed to save material, to make them lighter, and to make room for steel reinforcing bars.

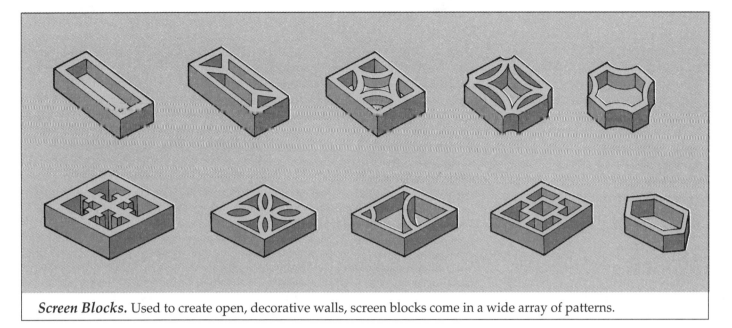

Screen Blocks. Used to create open, decorative walls, screen blocks come in a wide array of patterns.

stretcher. Stretchers are cored with two or three holes per unit to reduce the weight as much as possible. The core holes are tapered slightly to make it easier to remove them from the manufacturing molds and to provide a better grip for handling.

If your design will incorporate vertical reinforcing steel in the cores, the wall will be easier to build using special two-core units with open ends. These units are called A-blocks because they are shaped like the letter A. If A-blocks are not available from your supplier, you can make your own by sawing or knocking out the ends of regular units. This will let you place the blocks around the rebar rather than lifting and threading them over the top of the steel.

Screen Blocks. Screen blocks are used to create walls with open patterns. Walls can be made entirely of screen blocks, or a few courses of screen blocks can top a solid wall or be worked into the wall in several places. Screen blocks come in a variety of shapes and patterns.

Decorative Block. Another option is to build your wall with decorative block. These blocks come with one smooth face and one face with decorative ribs, geometric patterns or a rugged stone look. Because only one face is decorative, you must use two wythes of smaller blocks if you want a wall with a decorative finish on both sides. These units have the same face dimensions as an 8x16-inch block, but they are only $3\frac{5}{8}$ inches thick. Two wythes with a $\frac{3}{8}$-inch mortar joint in the middle measures $7\frac{5}{8}$ inches, which is the same as the actual thickness of the nominal 8-inch block. This makes it easy to finish the top of the wall with a nominal 8-inch cap block.

Interlocking Blocks. The interlocking retaining wall block is a fairly new type of concrete block material. There are several different types of systems marketed under a variety of trade names. They differ from traditional concrete block in that they are laid without mortar. Some systems interlock because of the shapes in which they are cast, some interlock with metal or plastic pins. The interlocking mechanisms also align the units correctly as they are stacked–it's like putting the pieces of a puzzle together. Building a retaining wall or a raised planter has never been easier. Some types of interlocking block can be used to build retaining walls as high as 12 feet. The manufacturers furnish step-by-step instructions tailored to the specific requirements of their units. A project using this material is presented later.

Estimating Materials Needed

Estimate the number of blocks you will need by multiplying the number of units in the wall length times the number of courses in the wall height. You can use units with flanged ends for most of the work, but at wall ends and corners, you will need units with flat ends. Unlike brick, which are wetted before using, concrete blocks must remain dry. Store them on-site in

Decorative Block. Two wythes of decorative block will give you a wall thickness equal to a single wythe of standard block.

a dry location, under plastic. Remember to include joint reinforcement and control joint blocks or building paper to create control joints. Estimate 6 cubic feet of mortar for every 100 square feet of wall surface. Refer to "Mortar," below, to estimate individual mortar ingredients.

Mortar

Both brick and concrete block are usually bonded together with mortar. Like concrete, masonry mortar contains cement, sand, and water. The difference is that concrete also contains gravel to increase its durability and compressive strength, while mortar usually contains hydrated lime to improve its working characteristics. With mortar, bond strength and workability are more important than compressive strength. Some types of concrete block retaining walls are "dry-stacked" without mortar. These units are interlocked mechanically with pins or simply lock together by shape.

The mortar in a masonry structure constitutes only a small percentage of the materials, but its importance cannot be overlooked. A good bond between the mortar and bricks or blocks provides stability, provides resistance to wind pressure and other lateral loads, and helps prevent moisture penetration. While mortar is similar to concrete, the kinds of mixtures that produce a good bond do not necessarily produce the high compressive strengths that are common with concrete mixes. As mentioned before, it is more important that mortar be workable and produce a good bond than have a high compressive strength.

Mortar and concrete typically use the same types of portland cement. The most common is a Type I general-purpose cement. Lime is added to mortar mixes to make them retain water longer, to improve workability or handling, and to make the hardened mortar less brittle and less prone to shrinkage. The mortar used

in historic buildings was made with lime and sand only, no portland cement. These lime mortars cured very slowly. The invention of portland cement in the late 1800s changed the way masonry mortar was made and speeded up construction. The trade-off is that the higher the portland cement content, the stiffer the mixture is when it is wet and the more rigid the mortar when it is cured. This makes the mortar a little harder to work with and a little more likely to crack if the masonry is not properly constructed.

There are two typical mortar mixes. For interior work, and outdoor work that is above grade, use a Type N mix. This mix is composed of 1 part portland cement, 1 part lime, and 6 parts sand. The lime should be a hydrated mason's lime, and the sand should be a well-graded masonry sand that has a range of grain sizes from fine to coarse. For below-grade construction and for paving projects, use a Type S mix. For flatwork, including patios, sidewalks, and driveways, an air-entrained portland cement will improve freeze-thaw resistance.

Mortar is usually mixed by volume proportions using a container of convenient size for consistent proportioning. Always use the same container for measuring ingredients so that the proportional volume of material is the same each time.

Ready-Mix Masonry Cements

Some manufacturers produce factory-blended masonry cements that are a combination either of portland cement and lime or of portland cement and natural or chemical agents. Masonry cements are available in Types N and S—these will produce a Type N or S mortar when mixed with sand in a one to three proportion (one part masonry cement to three parts sand). For small projects, masonry cements are more convenient than portland cement and lime mixes because all you have to do is add sand and water.

Masonry cements are also available with preblended pigments to produce a variety of mortar colors that range from white, cream, buff, tan, and pink to chocolate brown. This is the easiest way to get colored mortars, and it is easier to produce consistently colored batches than by mixing pigments separately. When buying masonry cements, read the label to make sure it meets the requirements of ASTM C91 Standard Specification for Masonry Cement.

For very small projects, you may find it most convenient to buy a mortar mix that includes both the masonry cement and the sand. These mixes are a bit more expensive than mixing your own, but they require only the

Portland Cement & Lime Mortars			
Mortar Type	Proportions By Volume		
	Portland Cement	Hydrated Mason's Lime	Mason's Sand
N	1	1	6
S	1	½	4½

Factory-Blended Masonry Cement Mortars		
Mortar Type	Proportions By Volume	
	Masonry Cement	Mason's Sand
N	1	3
S	1	3

addition of water at the project site. A packaged mortar mix is a practical option only for small projects, repairs, and repointing jobs.

See the charts, "Portland Cement and Limo Mortars" and "Factory Blended Masonry Cement Mortars" for proper mixing proportions.

Mixing Mortar

One of the most important things in mixing mortar is consistency from batch to batch. Always use a container for measuring ingredients so that the proportional volume of materials is the same each time. A 1- or 2-gallon plastic bucket is a good size, and not too heavy when it's filled.

If you're using a portland cement and lime mortar in a Type N 1:1:6 mixture, measure out one bucket of cement, one bucket of lime, and six buckets of sand; one bag of portland cement plus one bag of lime mortar mix will lay about 300 bricks or 75 blocks. If you're using a bagged masonry cement, measure out one bucket of cement and three buckets of sand. A single-bag masonry cement mix lays about 125 bricks or 30 blocks. For smaller batches, simply use a smaller bucket for measuring. Don't pack the materials in the bucket,

and don't mix more mortar than you can use in a couple of hours. You'll quickly get an idea of how much mortar you can lay before it sets up.

If you can't store materials close to where you'll be working, mix them in a wheelbarrow so you can move the mortar easily. When using a mortar box, make sure it is placed level so water won't collect in one end or in a corner.

First measure all of the dry ingredients and mix them thoroughly with a mason's hoe. If you put half the sand in first, then the cement and lime, and then add the rest of the sand, blending will be a little quicker and easier. Alternately pull and push the materials back and forth until the color is even. Then push the mix to one end of the mortar box or wheelbarrow, or make a hole in the middle. Pour 2 gallons of water in the empty end of the mixing box or the hole in the middle of the mortar mix; 2 gallons of water is about the right amount for one bag of portland cement and one bag of lime plus the sand. (Start with approximately 2 gallons when mixing masonry cement with sand.) Measure the water. Don't use a garden hose—it's too easy to put in too much water. Mix the dry ingredients with the water,

pushing and pulling the mix back and forth with a chopping motion until the consistency is uniform.

Adding Water. The amount of moisture in the sand will influence how much water you'll need to achieve the right mortar consistency. If you buy bags of sand for small projects, it will be dry. If you buy sand in bulk by the ton for larger projects, it will probably be damp or wet. (Keep your sand pile covered so that the moisture content will not change drastically with changes in the weather.) You're aiming for mortar that is the consistency of soft mud and will hold a ball shape. If the mix is too dry after the initial 2 gallons of water, add more water in small quantities until the consistency is right. To check for proper consistency, make a series of sharp ridges in the mortar with the hoe or trowel. If the ridges appear dry and crumbly, more water is needed. If the ridges stay sharp without slumping, the mortar is the right consistency. It is very easy to add too much water. If you put in too much, add proportional amounts of the dry ingredients to bring the mortar back to the proper consistency. This method is not as easy as adding water to a dry mix—so be careful when mixing.

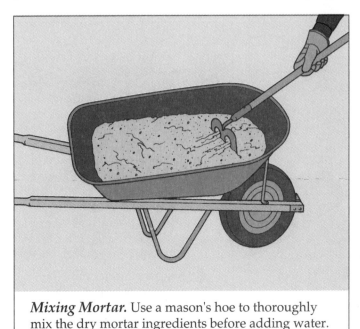

Mixing Mortar. Use a mason's hoe to thoroughly mix the dry mortar ingredients before adding water.

Adding Water. Make a series of sharp ridges in the mortar. The ridges should stay sharp without crumbling.

Within the first two hours after mixing, mortar can be retempered with water to replace evaporated moisture and restore proper consistency. In hot, dry weather, the time limits on retempering may be shorter. About 2½ hours after initial mixing, mortar begins to harden and must be discarded because it will never develop a good bond with the bricks or blocks. Don't retemper colored mortar because it will dilute the pigments and result in uneven colors in the wall. Mix smaller batches of colored mortar so you can use up batches more quickly.

How to Work with Mortar

If you have never worked with mortar before, you may want to practice a little before beginning your project. Slicing off a chunk of mortar and spreading it is a skill that is learned with practice. The key is holding the trowel correctly.

1 Setting up a Practice Surface. Lay a 2x4 flat across the top of two concrete blocks, buckets, or sawhorses. This is about the same width as a wythe of brick.

2 Using the Proper Grip. Grasp the trowel handle with your thumb extended on top of the handle, not over the end of it. Grip the handle firmly, but do not squeeze it.

3 Loading the Trowel. You can grab mortar directly from the mortar box or wheelbarrow by slicing a narrow V-shaped wedge of mortar with the trowel and lifting it out in a single scooping stroke away from your body. However, it is easier to place a small amount of mortar onto a hawk to then load the trowel. From the hawk, slice a piece off with the edge of the trowel and pull it away from the pile toward you. Scoop under to pick it up.

To keep the mortar from falling off the trowel before you're ready, "stick" it to the surface with a quick, slight snap of the wrist upward. Mortar of the correct consistency will not slide off.

4 Laying the Mortar. Hold the loaded trowel over the 2x4, and with a sweeping motion, turn it

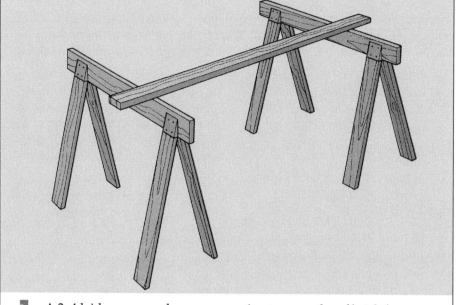

1 A 2x4 laid across sawhorses approximates a wythe of brick for practicing your mortaring technique.

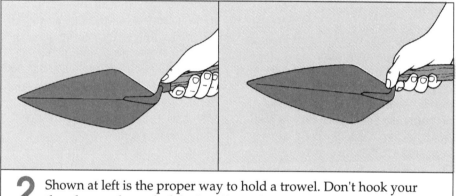

2 Shown at left is the proper way to hold a trowel. Don't hook your thumb over the end of the handle as shown at right.

3 Put some mortar on your hawk. Then quickly slice and scoop a trowel-load in one motion.

4 Snap the mortar onto the practice 2x4. Start with small amounts of mortar until you get the hang of it.

and snap the mortar out along the board. A full trowel-load of mortar is usually enough to lay three or four bricks or a couple of blocks. When you first begin, though, you may want to pick up smaller amounts. It will take some practice before this becomes a smooth motion and you are able to spread the mortar without throwing it off the sides of the board.

5 **Shaping the Mortar.** Use the edge of the trowel to cut off excess mortar at the sides of the 2x4. Then make a shallow furrow in the middle of the mortar bed. Don't make the furrow too deep.

Scrape the mortar off the 2x4 and return it to the batch, then repeat the steps until the feel of the trowel and the spreading motions become more comfortable.

Ties, Flashing, & Reinforcement

Masonry construction usually requires accessory items such as ties to bond multiple wythes of masonry, flashing to limit water penetration, and reinforcement for lateral strength.

Ties. Multiple wythes of masonry in a wall must be tied together either with

5 Make a shallow furrow in the middle of the mortar bed to help spread the mortar when you place the bricks.

header bricks or metal ties. Header bricks are laid perpendicular to the wall length, overlapping both wythes and creating a pattern bond in the wall surface. Metal ties can be used in walls of parallel, unconnected wythes. The ties are imbedded in the mortar to join wythes. A Z-shaped wire tie is used for solid masonry units such as brick; a rectangular wire tie is used for hollow masonry units such as concrete block or to tie

concrete block and brick wythes together. Rectangular ties and Z-ties are $3/16$ inch in diameter. For extra protection against corrosion, use ties that are hot-dip galvanized.

Veneer Walls. Brick can be used as a nonload-bearing wall veneer. The wall is built 1 inch away from the house sheathing. If the framing is wooden, the brick can be attached to the structure with corrugated veneer anchors. Anchors are connected to wood framing, metal studs, or concrete at every 16 inches vertically and every 32 inches horizontally.

Reinforcement. There are two types of masonry reinforcement. The first is a prefabricated wire joint reinforcement that is used primarily in the mortar beds of concrete block walls to help control shrinkage cracking. For residential projects, the side wires should be a 9-gauge thickness. The width of the joint reinforcement should always be about 1 inch less than the width of the blocks so that it is covered on each side of the wall with $1/2$ to $5/8$ inch of mortar.

The second type of masonry reinforcement is heavy steel reinforcing bars like those used in concrete construction. Called

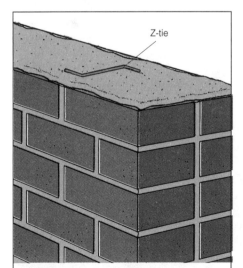

Ties. Z-ties are used to bond wythes together. Use ties that have been hot-dipped galvanized for protection against corrosion.

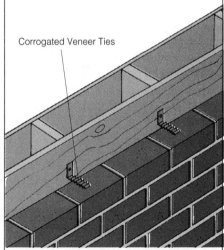

Veneer Walls. Nonload-bearing brick veneer walls are connected to wood framing with corrugated veneer ties.

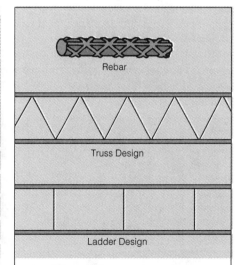

Reinforcement. Wire reinforcement is laid in mortar beds. Steel reinforcing bar is usually required only in supporting members.

rebar, these bars are used in masonry to strengthen supporting members such as piers, lintels, and bond beams.

Masonry ties, anchors, and joint reinforcement should always be placed in the mortar bed rather than lain on the unit. This will provide better embedment of the metal and better performance of the masonry.

Flashing. Masonry flashing can be made of metal, rubberized asphalt sheet membranes, or other materials. It is used to control moisture in masonry walls either by keeping the top of a wall dry or by collecting water inside a wall so that it can be drained out through weep holes.

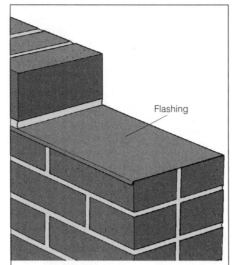

Flashing. Masonry flashing is used to keep water out of walls or to direct it to weep holes.

Brick Terminology

To understand the procedures in this book, you must first learn some terminology used by masons. Like any trade, there are a few terms that are specific to the craft.

As mentioned before, a wythe is a vertical section of a wall that is one masonry unit thick. Typical brick garden walls are two wythes thick. Another basic term is course. A course is simply a horizontal row of a masonry units. A garden wall

4 feet tall has 18 courses of 2¼-inch-thick bricks plus mortar joints.

Brick Positions. A brick that is laid lengthwise in the course is called a stretcher. When standing upright with the edge facing out, the brick is called a soldier, when the face is positioned out, a sailor. A stretcher unit that is rotated 90 degrees in a wall so that the end is facing out is called a header. If the unit is then stood on its edge, it's called a rowlock. With modular brick, no matter which way you turn the units, they will work to a 4-inch module. A header unit is exactly the same width as a wall built of two wythes of brick with a ⅜-inch mortar joint in between. Concrete blocks are normally laid only in the stretcher position. As you will see, using alternating stretcher and header units, you can easily create patterns and designs in a wall—called the wall's bond pattern.

Joint Positions. Horizontal joints are called bed joints, vertical joints

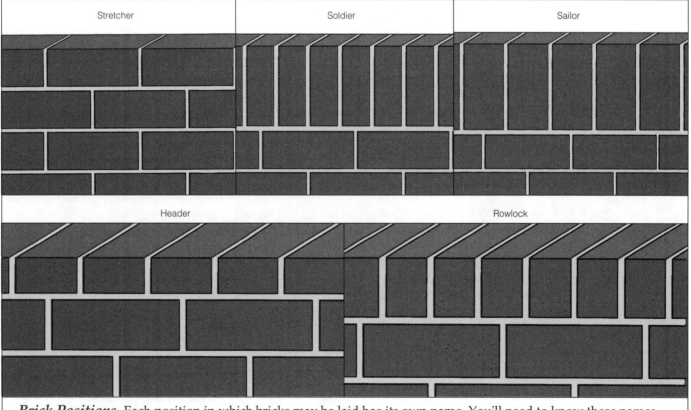

Brick Positions. Each position in which bricks may be laid has its own name. You'll need to know these names to understand descriptions of brick patterns.

between individual bricks or blocks are called head joints, and the vertical joint between wythes is called a collar joint.

Partial Bricks. A brick cut in half longthwise is called a bat. One that is halved in width is called a soap, and one that halved in height is called a split.

Expansion Joints

Allowances must be made in masonry construction for expansion and contraction. All construction materials, including brick and block masonry, expand and contract with changes in temperature. Clay brick also expands with the absorption of moisture; concrete masonry shrinks with loss of residual moisture from the manufacturing and construction process.

To prevent cracking from expansion and contraction, masonry walls are built with vertical expansion joints (for brick walls) and control joints (for block walls). A masonry expansion joint is a soft, mortarless joint that is designed to accommodate the natural expansion of brick. The exact locations are dictated by design features, such as openings, offsets, and intersections. In brick walls, expansion joints are located near corners because the opposing push of intersecting walls can cause cracking. For both brick and concrete masonry walls, joints should be located at points of weakness or high stress concentration, such as abrupt changes in wall height, changes in wall thickness, at columns and piers, and at one or both sides of windows

and doors. Short freestanding walls that are not connected to other structures may not require control or expansion joints, as they can expand and contract independently.

Locating Expansion and Control Joints. If you are working with a wall that is more than 30 feet long, you will need to install at least one expansion joint. If either end of the wall is built against an existing structure such as a house, garage, or other wall, install an expansion joint between the two elements. If the wall is long and straight, place expansion joints no more than 30 feet apart. For L- and U-shaped walls, locate expansion joints near the corners.

There are several ways to build control joints in concrete block walls. The most common methods are illustrated in the concrete block garden wall project. See page 46.

Installing Expansion Joints. Make an expansion joint ⅜ to ½ inch wide. To keep mortar from accidentally blocking the joint during construction, fill the joint with a soft foam pad or piece of ⅜- or ½-inch plywood. The foam pad will stay in place; the plywood will be removed. If you use a foam pad, be sure its edges are recessed from the wall face about ¾ inch so that you can caulk the joint with silicone sealant (matched to your mortar color), after the wall is finished. Continue the expansion joint up through the wall cap or coping.

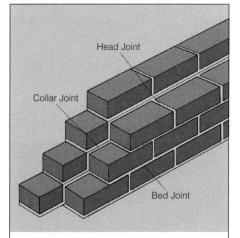

Joint Positions. Like the bricks, joints also are named according to their positions in the wall.

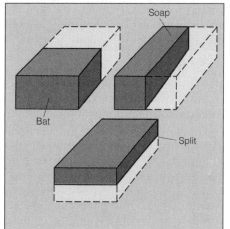

Partial Bricks. Bat, soap, and split describe the three ways you can cut a brick in half.

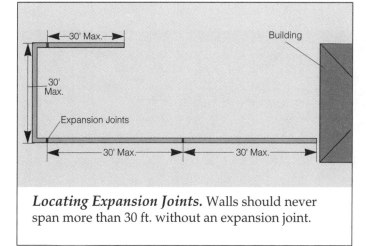

Locating Expansion Joints. Walls should never span more than 30 ft. without an expansion joint.

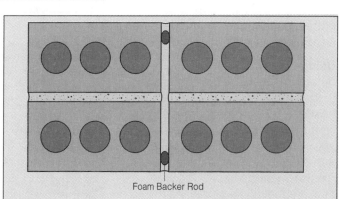

Installing Expansion Joints. These flexible joints are made with foam backer rod and sealed with silicone caulk.

Remember to install a foam backer rod to form the back side of the caulked joint. Buy closed-cell backer rods and silicone sealant from a building supply company. Smooth the surface of the sealant to compress it firmly into the joint.

Steel joint reinforcement can also be used to restrain movement and reduce the number of control or expansion joints needed. This reinforcement is routinely used in concrete block walls to reduce shrinkage and is also sometimes used in brick walls to control expansion. For concrete block walls, prefabricated wire reinforcement is usually placed in every second or third bed joint.

Bond Patterns for Walls

The pattern in which the bricks are laid is called the bond. The most common bond is one where bricks are laid flat on their widest surface and turned lengthwise in the wall in the stretcher position. Each brick in a course of stretchers (a horizontal row) is offset one-half brick from the bricks in the course above and below. The pattern formed by overlapping the brick in this way is called a running bond. If the bricks are offset one-third or one-quarter brick in each course, the pattern is called a one-third or one-quarter running bond, and the appearance differs slightly. The running bond pattern goes well in any landscape and is easy to keep consistent.

Using Headers. As mentioned before, bricks turned perpendicular to the stretcher courses are called headers. By alternating header and stretcher bricks in different ways, you can create a variety of patterns, and since header units help hold the two wythes of a wall together, they are functional as well as decorative. There are a number of decorative bond patterns that mimic the look of historic masonry buildings, so the style goes well with older homes and with new homes of traditional design.

Popular Bonds. The common, or American, bond is similar to the running bond, except it has courses of headers spaced every sixth course. The English bond consists of alternating courses of stretchers and headers; the headers are centered over the stretchers, and the vertical joints of all the stretcher courses align. A stack bond lays all the bricks as either headers or stretchers with all joints aligning vertically. The stack bond requires great precision to lay correctly and is used for veneer surfaces only— it is not permitted for load-bearing or structural walls. The Flemish bond is a complex pattern in which every course has alternating stretchers and headers. The pattern is offset by courses so that the headers center over stretchers and vice versa.

Bond Patterns for Walls. The most common pattern for walls of brick or stretcher blocks is the running bond.

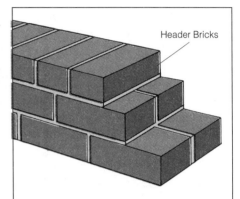

Header Bricks

Using Headers. Bricks are placed in the header position to tie wythes together and to create decorative bonds.

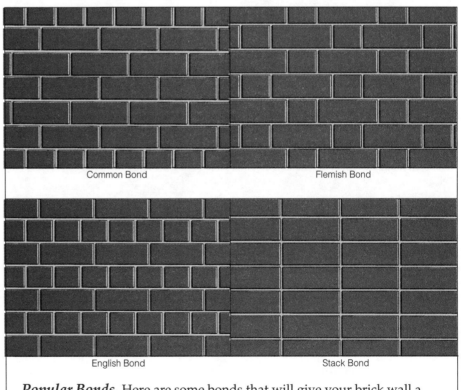

Common Bond

Flemish Bond

English Bond

Stack Bond

Popular Bonds. Here are some bonds that will give your brick wall a distinctive look.

BUILDING BRICK WALLS

This chapter provides step-by-step instructions for a double-wythe brick garden wall, and a gently curving brick wall. These two projects provide all the information you'll need to design and build your own brick wall. You'll also find ideas for embellishing your wall with your own creative touches.

Brick Garden Wall

You don't need to be an experienced mason to build an attractive brick garden wall. You'll quickly learn the necessary skills as you go, and as you become more proficient with a trowel and mortar, your work will get faster and more efficient.

A brick garden wall can provide privacy for a patio, define the perimeters of a lawn or garden area, or screen out street noise. Brick walls can be built in a vast array of styles to suit any landscape. The most common type of garden wall is two wythes thick and laid with the brick in straight, parallel rows in a running bond pattern. A double-wythe brick wall has a finished thickness of about 8 inches, which provides enough stiffness for a wall height of at least 6 feet. This is the maximum that most building codes allow without reinforcing steel. Remember to include expansion joints every 30 feet, near corners, and where the wall abuts existing construction.

Drainage. Study the slopes and drainage patterns in your yard to make sure the wall will not dam natural storm water runoff paths. If necessary, reshape the ground to drain water away from the wall.

Laying Out the Wall. Planning the wall layout will be easiest if you use a modular-size brick: 7⅝ inches long, 3⅝ inches wide, and 2¼ inches thick when laid flat as a stretcher. When laid in the wall with standard ⅜-inch mortar joints, the nominal length is 8 inches, and the nominal width is 4 inches. Since three courses of bricks with mortar joints measure 8 inches high, all your dimensions can be planned as multiples of 4 inches (the nominal length of half a brick). Using a piece of graph paper, draw a plan of the wall to scale, making each brick twice as long as it is wide. Draw the plan of the wall using only whole and half bricks.

Also draw a side view, or elevation, of the wall. Figure three courses of modular brick with horizontal mortar

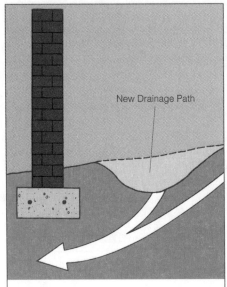

Drainage. You may have to reshape the ground around your wall so you don't dam natural runoff paths.

joints for every 8 inches of height. This would mean that a 4-foot-high wall has 18 courses of brick, and a 6-foot-high wall has 27 courses.

Adding Pilasters for Strength.

Masonry walls must have supporting pilasters to keep them from falling over. Pilasters are thicker wall sections added at regular intervals to add stiffness to the wall. Factors such as the wall's height and the wind pressure exerted on the wall dictate the placement of pilasters. The usual spacing of pilasters is at a distance 18 times the thickness of the wall. Follow this guideline if you are building a wall less than 6 feet high with a continuous concrete reinforced footing. This means that a 4-inch-thick unreinforced masonry wall must have pilasters every 72 inches (18 times 4 inches = 72 inches). An 8-inch-thick wall would require pilasters every 12 feet, and a 12-inch-thick wall every 18 feet. Check with your local building department to find out what the rules are in your area. If you live in an area that is subject to earthquake activity, you should use a special seismic design and will need the services of a structural engineer.

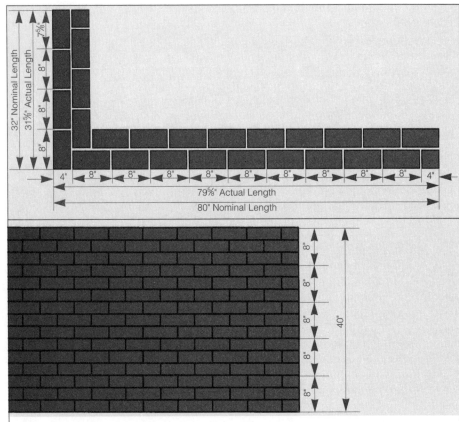

Laying Out the Wall. Use a piece of graph paper to make scale drawing of your wall layout. Do an elevation view as well.

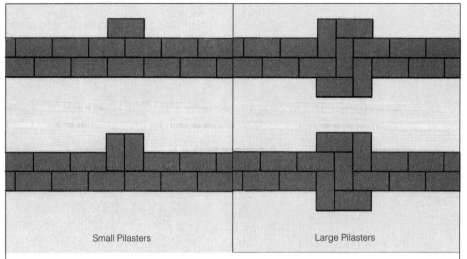

Small Pilasters

Large Pilasters

Adding Pilasters for Strength. You must include thicker wall sections called pilasters to make walls strong enough to withstand strong winds without toppling.

In a short wall, pilasters can be used as decorative features even when they're not needed for extra strength—because they break up the line of a brick wall. Small pilasters can be built to project on only one side of the wall; larger pilasters can project on both sides. The small pilasters are adequate for walls up to 4 feet high, and the large ones for walls up to 6 feet high. Alternating courses of brick in the wall must overlap the brick in the pilaster to form a strong interlocking structure.

Designing the Footing. Brick walls need a concrete footing for stability and support. The thickness of the footing is the same as the width of the wall. The concrete footing must be twice as wide as the wall's width. For an 8-inch-wide double-wythe wall, the footing is 16 inches wide. Remember that the footing must expand in width around any pilasters. If you are building along a property line, the full footing width must be inside your property line. If you are building adjacent to an existing patio or sidewalk, plan ahead so the full width of the footing can be poured next to the existing slab with a small space in between to separate the two.

Considering Frost Depth. The footing must be built below the frost depth so that it will not heave or tilt when the soil freezes and thaws each year. For footings that must be set very deep, it is much more economical to first build a concrete wall on the footing up to ground level rather than building many courses of brick below the ground surface. See "Concrete Footings," on page 10.

Stepping Down Slopes. If the ground slopes substantially along the length of the wall, both the concrete footing and the brick wall may have to be stepped to follow the slope. Stepped footings are also described under "Concrete Footings." For flatter slopes, build a footing that is deep enough so that its bottom is below the frost line and its top is level for the full length of the wall.

Marking the Wall on the Footing

The following project is an example of how to build a two-wythe brick wall with a corner. The wall uses a running bond pattern, the easiest-to-build and most common style. The sample wall section starts near a garage and runs 35 feet, turns 90 degrees, and runs another 20 feet. The wall is 4 feet high,

Brick Wall

Concrete Wall Below Ground Level

Wall Thickness

Rebar

Equals Wall Thickness

Equals Twice Wall Thickness

Designing the Footing. Footings should be twice as wide as the wall and as thick as the wall is wide.

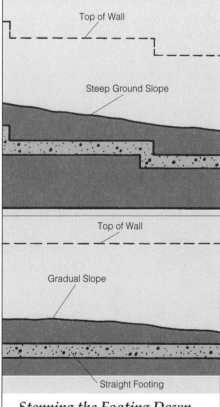

Top of Wall

Steep Ground Slope

Top of Wall

Gradual Slope

Straight Footing

Stepping the Footing Down Slopes. A steep slope requires a stepped footing.

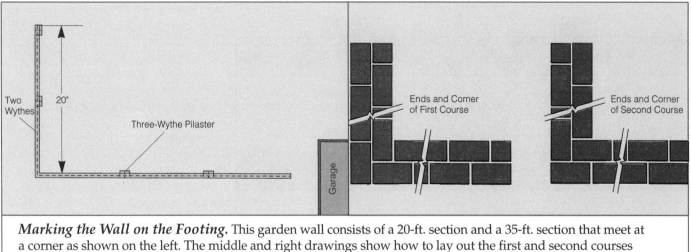

Two Wythes

20"

Three-Wythe Pilaster

Garage

Ends and Corner of First Course

Ends and Corner of Second Course

Marking the Wall on the Footing. This garden wall consists of a 20-ft. section and a 35-ft. section that meet at a corner as shown on the left. The middle and right drawings show how to lay out the first and second courses at the corner.

so it has 18 courses of bricks. The wall is built with brick measuring a nominal 4x8 inches, so in the outside wythe, the 35-foot-courses contain 52½ bricks, and the 20-foot courses contain 30 bricks. The inside wythe measures one half brick less for each course. As for placing the pilasters, 18 times the thickness of the wall (8 inches) equals 12 feet. This wall needs pilasters at a spacing of no greater than every 12 feet. Aesthetically, the wall will look best if the pilasters are evenly spaced at shorter distances. It's fine to use spacings shorter than required. In this sample project, there is no pilaster at the corner so that you can learn how to interlock a running bond corner. However, you might like the way the wall looks if you include a pilaster at the corner. As a plus, the wall will be a bit stronger, too.

This project begins after you've plotted the site and built the concrete footing for the wall. See "Concrete Footings" on page 10 for how to do this.

1 Snapping a Chalk Line. After your concrete footing has cured for at least seven days, brush all debris from the surface. Measure and mark the location of the outside face of the wall, being careful to center the masonry across the width of the footing. For an 8-inch-wide wall on a 16-inch-wide footing, simply measure 4 inches in from the footing edge at both ends of the wall and snap a line between these measurements to mark the outside face of the wall.

Estimating Materials Needed

Estimate the number of bricks you will need by multiplying the number of units in the wall length times the number of courses in the wall height. For decorative bond patterns, draw an elevation of the wall to scale on graph paper, and then count the number of stretcher and header units. Remember that for double-wythe walls, you must double the number of stretcher units to account for the two wythes. Estimate 28 cubic feet of mortar for every 100 square feet of wall surface. Refer to "Mortar" to estimate individual mortar ingredients. See page 24.

4"

1 Snap a chalk line to indicate the front of the wall.

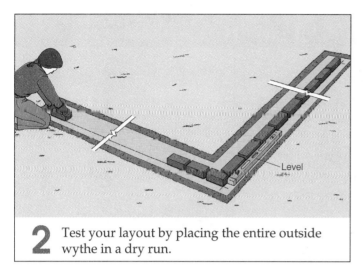

2 Test your layout by placing the entire outside wythe in a dry run.

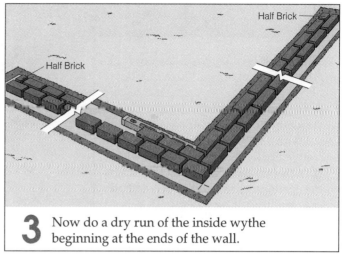

Half Brick

Half Brick

3 Now do a dry run of the inside wythe beginning at the ends of the wall.

As with the footing, batter boards and string are used to determine the corner locations. Square the corners and snap a chalk line along the length of the footing. To ensure that the corners are square, use the 3-4-5 triangle method. From the outside corner point, measure up 4 feet along one leg of the footing, and 3 feet along the other leg. The two lines are square when the diagonal between the two points measures 5 feet. To square the line of a wall against an existing wall, again use the 3-4-5 triangle method.

2 Laying the Outside Wythe in a Dry Run. Check the wall length and design by laying out a dry course of brick. Lay the outside wythe of bricks as stretchers along the chalk line. Start at one end, lay a few bricks without mortar, then move to the other end. Use whole bricks and fill in toward the middle. Use a small scrap of ⅜-inch plywood to space the units. Adjust the size of the joints between the ends of the bricks (called head joints) to make up for slight variations in the size of the bricks. Every brick and head joint combination should be 8 inches long. If you are using rough or antiqued brick, which varies more in size, you will have to take up the slack at the joints to achieve the correct overall length. Use the edge of a level to periodically check for proper alignment along the chalk line. When you

get to the middle of the wall, go back to the other end and complete the dry run of the outside wythe.

3 Laying the Inside Wythe in a Dry Run. Now lay out the stretchers of the inside wythe parallel to the outside wythe. Begin at the ends, using half-bricks, and allow about ⅜ inch between the two wythes for a collar joint. Notice that the head joints are offset by a half brick length in the two wythes. This makes the wall stronger than if the joints were aligned. If your wall is straight and does not have a corner, lay out the inside wythe beginning and ending with a half brick to create this same offset. Remember to lay the pilasters where indicated on your layout.

4 Marking the Joint Locations. Adjust the head joints if necessary for even spacing, and mark the joint locations on the footing when all the bricks are dry laid. Using a marker, pencil, or chalk, make long slash marks at all the joints so that you will be able to confirm the spacing of the first course as you work. Make some type of distinctive mark to locate expansion joints. Check the wall width periodically by laying a header brick perpendicular to the stretchers. The width of the wall should be exactly the same as the length of the header brick.

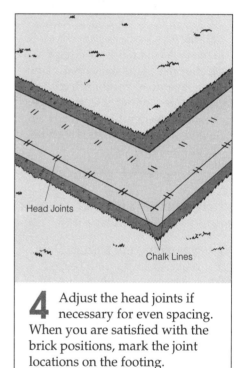

Head Joints

Chalk Lines

4 Adjust the head joints if necessary for even spacing. When you are satisfied with the brick positions, mark the joint locations on the footing.

Creating the Brick Leads

After marking the joints and moving the dry run bricks out of the way, you'll begin wall construction by building leading sections, or leads, at the ends and corners. Masonry walls are always laid from the ends first and filled in toward the middle; the leads help establish the correct spacing and coursing heights for the rest of the wall. The first course of a corner or end lead for a brick wall should be from three to five bricks long. The second and successive courses are set back one-half brick

Cutting Bricks in Advance

The wall shown here will use only whole and half bricks. Cut a number of half bricks now so you won't have to stop and start during wall construction. Soft brick can usually be cut with a quick downward blow from a brick hammer. Experienced masons can split bricks exactly using this technique. However, this method may be difficult for a novice. A better technique is to place the brick on firm ground, score it on all four sides with a brickset, then sever the brick with a final sharp blow.

Hard brick, such as pavers, can be cut with a circular saw equipped with a masonry blade. Be sure to clamp the paver to a workbench and wear eye protection when cutting. For even quicker cutting, you can rent a mechanical cutter, called a guillotine, at a tool-rental shop.

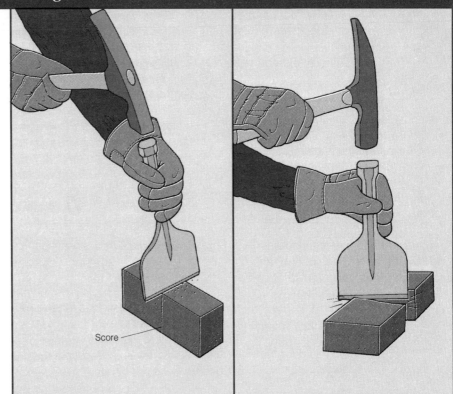

Score

length in each course when using the running bond pattern.

1 Spreading the Mortar. Mix a batch of mortar and begin the first course of the lead at either the corner or one end of the wall. Pick up a trowel-load of mortar and spread it along the chalk line on the footing. Use enough mortar to make a bed joint that is ½ to ¾ inch thick (slightly wider than a brick) and two or three bricks long. This first course is critical–you want to lay enough mortar so that when you place the bricks, the bed joint doesn't develop voids.

2 Laying the First Brick. Lay the corner or end unit first, pressing it firmly down into the mortar. Measure to make sure the mortar bed is the right thickness (about ⅜ inch) so that the brick is at the right height. Tap the unit lightly with the trowel handle, if necessary, to settle the brick. If the

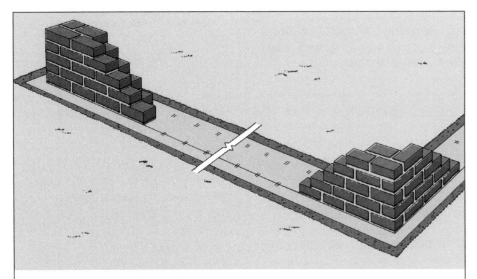

Creating the Brick Leads. You'll start construction by building up the corners, called the leads.

1 Spread enough mortar to set two or three bricks.

footing surface is uneven, vary the thickness of this first bed joint along its length to keep the brick course level.

3 Buttering the Head Joint.
Put mortar on the end of the next brick by holding it in one hand and swiping mortar onto it from all four directions. Make sure you get enough mortar to form a full ⅜-inch joint between this and the adjacent brick.

Press the second brick down into the mortar bed and against the first brick, making a tight joint. Don't push too hard against the other brick or you will dislodge it and break the mortar bond—but press firmly enough to squeeze mortar from both the head and bed joints. If the mortar doesn't squeeze out, there isn't enough mortar in the joints. After laying each brick, trowel off excess mortar at the face of the wall. Lay the first course of both wythes of your lead.

4 Installing Metal Ties.
Since the running bond pattern includes no bricks that overlap both wythes, you will need to connect the two wythes with metal ties. Install the first row of ties in the bed joint between the first and second course of brick. Make sure that each tie is properly embedded, with mortar completely surrounding it on all sides. Spread the mortar first, make the furrow, and then place the ties. Press them down into the middle of the mortar, and then add a little mortar on top to cover.

The ties most commonly used to connect two wythes of brick are 7-shaped rigid wire ties. Most building codes require that rigid wire ties be spaced 18 inches on-center vertically (every eighth course of brick) and 36 inches on-center horizontally. Every other row of ties should be offset to create a staggered pattern.

5 Filling the Collar Joint with Each Course.
Be sure to completely fill the collar joint between wythes as you go. Place the mortar for the collar joint as each course is set; use the tip of the trowel to make sure the mortar fills the joint without voids. Do not push the bricks out of plumb when putting mortar in the collar joint. Check the courses with a 4-foot level to verify plumb and level. Also, hold a story pole that is marked every 8 inches up to the lead to quickly check the correct height of the courses.

6 Finishing the Leads.
Lay the rest of your leads, raking back one-half brick in each course to establish the bond pattern. A 4-foot

2
Set the first corner brick, tapping it lightly, if necessary, to set it into the mortar.

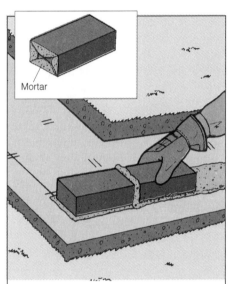

Mortar

3
To make the head joint, put mortar on the side of the brick, swiping from four sides.

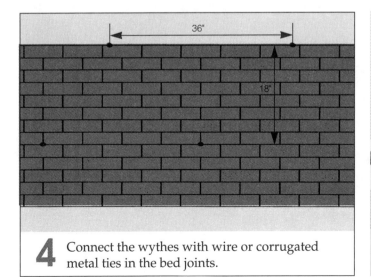

36"

18"

4
Connect the wythes with wire or corrugated metal ties in the bed joints.

Story Pole

Collar Joint

5
As you build each course, be sure to fill the collar joint with mortar.

level or straight 2x4 laid carefully along the slope, or "rack," of the lead should touch the corner of each brick.

6 Finish the lead, making each course a half brick shorter than the course below to establish the running bond.

Preparing Line Blocks

To fill in the masonry between leads, you need to stretch a string line to mark each course as you build up the wall. Use line blocks and mason's twine to do this. (Mason's twine is better than cotton string because it will stretch tight without sagging.) Secure the twine by first pulling it through the slot in the middle of the block and wrapping it around the right side of the block. Pull the line through the center slot again and wrap the line around the left block. Hook the block around a corner brick and stretch the twine to the opposite corner. Pull the twine tight in the slot of the other block, hook it around the block edges, and secure it around a corner brick of the same course. The line must not sag in the middle.

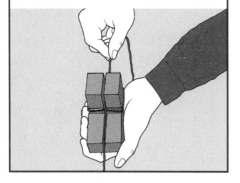

Tooling Mortar Joints

As you lay the bricks, you'll remove excess mortar from the face of the joints with the edge of the trowel blade. After the mortar has begun to cure, however, the surfaces of the head and bed joints need to be tooled to compress the mortar and to decrease moisture absorption at the surface. It is important that joints be tooled at a consistent moisture content so that they do not appear light in some areas and dark in others. The joints are ready for tooling when the mortar is "thumb-print" hard. This means that you can press your thumb against the mortar and leave a print impression without any mortar sticking to your thumb. The concave joint is most commonly used today. The concave, V, and grapevine joints are most weather-resistant because the surface of the mortar is compacted as it is tooled.

Concave joints make for a flat wall appearance, where this is desired. V joints emphasize shadows. Flush joints are acceptable in areas not subject to heavy amounts of rain. Raked joints leave the mortar perpendicular and recessed almost ½ inch; these joints create dark shadows. Beaded joints have a formal appearance and create strong shadow lines. Struck joints and weathered joints also create dark lines on the wall. Joint types can be mixed. For example, you may combine flush vertical joints with beaded horizontal joints to produce long horizontal shadows. However, mixing joint styles in a pleasing manner is difficult to do, even for a professional.

Joint shapes are created using different tools. Using the correct jointing tool for the shape you have selected, tool the head joints first and then the bed joints—this will leave a smooth, unbroken line on the bed joints. Don't wait until you have finished a large section of wall before you tool the joints. Check the mortar frequently, and tool the joints a few at a time when the surface is just the

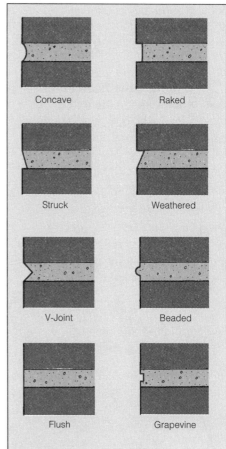

Tooling Mortar Joints. Jointing tools are available in various shapes to provide a variety of joint styles.

Mortar Joints. Tool all the head joints before tooling the bed joints with one stroke.

right consistency. As the joints are tooled, small pieces of mortar called "tailings" will be squeezed out at the edges of the joints. Remove these with the edge of the trowel.

Filling between Leads

1 **Setting the String Line.** Hook one line block on the corner of the lead so that the string is level with the top of the brick in the course you're working on. Stretch the string to the opposite corner lead and hook the other line block at the same height. Check the line with a line level. The line blocks hold the string about ⅟₁₆ inch away from the face of the wall. The masonry in between the leads can now be "laid to the line" to keep the wall straight and the brick course level.

2 **Filling in First Course.** Fill in the first course between leads, checking the face of the bricks to make sure they are correctly laid along the chalk line and with the proper head joint thickness. Work on the outside wythe first. It is critical that the first course of brick be level and plumb, because it is the base for the entire wall. You can correct slight irregularities in the concrete footing by varying the thickness of the first mortar bed, up to a maximum of about ¾ inch. You can allow for slight variations in brick length by adjusting the thickness of the head joints between the ends of the units, but try to keep the head joints fairly uniform in size. Remember to account for any expansion joints in a wall over 30 feet long. See "Expansion Joints," on page 29.

3 **Laying the Closure Unit.** The last brick to be put into place in a course is called a *closure brick*. You should have just enough space left for this brick plus a head joint on each end. To make sure you get full head joints, butter the ends of the adjacent units and butter both ends of the closure brick. Lower the brick into place from above, being careful not to dislodge the adjacent bricks.

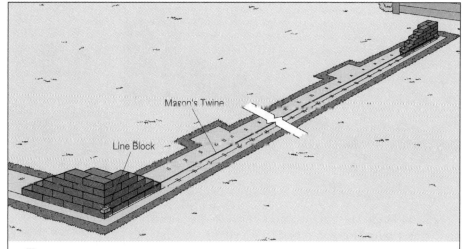

1 The line block will keep the string taut and about 1/16 inch away from the wall so you can lay brick accurately to the line.

2 Fill in the wall, working on the outside wythe first. Be especially careful to get the first course straight and level.

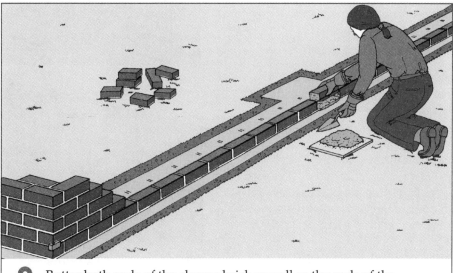

3 Butter both ends of the closure brick as well as the ends of the adjacent bricks.

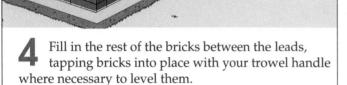

4 Fill in the rest of the bricks between the leads, tapping bricks into place with your trowel handle where necessary to level them.

5 If your wall will continue higher, begin again with new leads, filling them in just as you did between the first leads.

Now complete the inside wythe of the wall. Completely fill between the wythes with mortar.

Note: Remember that ties will begin here, on top of the first course.

4 Completely Filling between Leads. As you work on successive courses, continually check the tops of the brick with a 4-foot level to make sure that each course is level. Tap down any bricks that are set too high. Remove bricks that are set too low, cut away the mortar, and lay the unit with fresh mortar. Any brick that is dislodged after it is initially set must be removed, the mortar cut away, and the unit relaid with fresh mortar. Also check that the bricks are plumb. Use the side of the level as a straightedge to align the face of the units in each course.

5 Building Up New Leads. When you have filled in the courses between your leads, build up the ends or corners of the walls again to form new leads. Continue to place the ties and fill the collar joint just as you did in the first section of wall. Repeat the process of filling in courses and building up leads until you reach the final wall height.

Installing a Wall Coping

When the wall is at the final height, the top is finished with a final course called the coping. Coping on a brick wall ties the masonry units together and helps retard water penetration. When water penetrates the joints, it can freeze and do severe damage to a masonry structure. The coping can be a course of rowlock header bricks, stone slabs, or specially molded brick or concrete units. For this project, a rowlock coping is used. For the course immediately below the coping, use solid brick without cores, or fill the cores with mortar. It is also important that the collar joint between the wythes be entirely filled to eliminate voids in which water could collect and freeze.

1 Installing Flashing. For maximum weather protection, install flashing immediately below the wall coping. Stainless steel flashing

Installing a Wall Coping. Wall copings vary in style but they all are designed to tie the top of the wall together while preventing water from penetrating the wall.

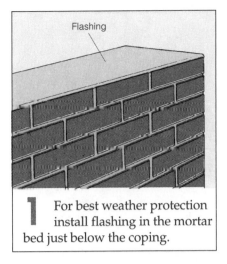

1 For best weather protection install flashing in the mortar bed just below the coping.

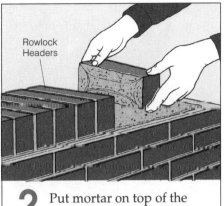

2 Put mortar on top of the flashing and lay the coping in the mortar.

is the most resistant to corrosion. Copper flashing also resists ordinary corrosion, provides an excellent moisture barrier, and is easy to shape. To save money, you can also use self-adhesive rubberized asphalt flashing, or a plastic flashing that is rated as resistant to degradation from ultraviolet light, or a laminated combination flashing.

Place a thin bed of mortar on top of the wall, center the flashing over the two wythes, and press it down into the mortar. Work with relatively short sections of flashing (about 4 feet), so your mortar doesn't dry out, and overlap the flashing sections about 4 to 6 inches. Seal lap joints with nonhardening mastic or caulk. If you are using metal flashing, extend it ½ inch or so beyond the faces of the wall and turn it down to form a drip edge. Flexible flashings won't hold a bend, so extend them past the wall and later trim them flush with the joint.

2 **Laying the Coping.** Lay a bed of mortar on top of the flashing, then butter one side of your coping units and lay them as the top course of the wall. If you are using brick, lay the bricks on edge in the rowlock position to form a brick coping. Use solid bricks without cores at the ends where the side of the brick is exposed. Make sure the joints are completely filled and then tooled to compress the surface of the mortar. Check for level and alignment by holding a 4-foot level to the rowlocks.

Cleaning the Wall. After the wall has set for about a week, brush the surface with a stiff natural- or synthetic-bristle brush to remove mortar drips and dust. Use a plastic or wooden scraper and then a brush to remove large mortar splatters. If necessary, clean completed red brick walls with a diluted solution of muriatic acid (mixed 1:10 with water). Don't use muriatic acid on white, cream, buff, gray, or brown brick because it can leave ugly green or brown stains–check with the brick manufacturer or distributor. Before applying an acid cleaning solution, thoroughly wet the wall with a garden hose. Wearing rubber gloves, apply the acid solution carefully with a special acid brush available from masonry suppliers. Scrub lightly, then thoroughly rinse the wall with the garden hose. Be extremely careful when working with acid to avoid burns and other injuries. Don't use metal tools or buckets because the acid will corrode them. Always pour the water in the bucket first, then add the acid.

Making Corners for Decorative Bonds

The project just described was built with a running bond pattern, however, you may prefer a decorative bond pattern that requires some extra planning. In a double-wythe wall with a decorative bond pattern, brick headers will connect the wythes instead of metal ties. Refer to "Bond Patterns for Walls," on page 30, for details.

Common Bond. The common bond pattern uses header units in every sixth course. With common bond, it is customary to begin with a header course at the base of the wall; one-quarter and three-quarter closure units are required to make the corner pattern. It is important to build the inside and outside wythes at the

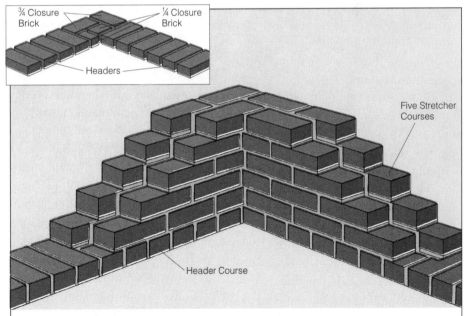

Common Bond. The corner for the common bond requires three-quarter and one-quarter closure bricks.

same time so that the header units can be set in place properly. The long joints between header units should be buttered with mortar as you would normally butter a head joint between stretchers. Hold the brick in one hand and scrape mortar onto the side with the trowel from all four directions, making sure you get enough mortar to completely fill the joint. Be sure also to completely fill the collar joint between stretcher wythes as each course is laid so that the wall is the same thickness as the length of the header units.

Flemish Bond. The Flemish bond pattern uses alternating stretcher and header units in every course. There are two ways of forming the corner pattern for a Flemish bond wall. One is called a Dutch corner and uses cut half-length and three-quarter-length units. The other option is called an English corner, which uses a field-cut closure brick called a queen closure.

Flemish Bond. The Flemish bond can be built with a Dutch corner, as shown at the top, or with an English corner, as shown at the bottom.

Labels on image: Whole Brick; Half Bricks; ¾ Bricks; Queen Closure

---

Additional Waterproofing

Before filling in the excavated area around the base of the wall, the bricks below ground must be treated against moisture penetration. There are two methods for doing this.

The first and easiest method involves brushing on a heavy bituminous coating that is composed of asphaltic materials. The coating is applied as if it were thick paint. Use an old throwaway brush or roller. Do not go above ground as the black tar-like coating is unattractive.

The second method is to parge (coat) the bricks below ground with a ¼-inch layer of cement plaster to form a protective shield against moisture. Trowel on the cement as you would apply plaster to a wall.

Either method is effective. Once completed and dried as according to the manufacturer's directions, fill in the excavation and tamp the soil solidly.

Serpentine Brick Wall

A serpentine, or S-shaped, brick wall is both unusual and attractive. It is a style made famous by Thomas Jefferson in the gardens that he designed at the University of Virginia in Charlottesville.

While most brick walls require a double thickness of brick for strength and stability, serpentine walls can be built with a single wythe of units because of the curved shape. If you try to stand a piece of cardboard on its edge, it will fall over; but if you fold or bend the cardboard into an S or a zigzag, it will stand up by itself. This same principle permits the use of single-wythe brick for building serpentine walls.

The brick-laying technique for a serpentine wall is the same as the previous brick garden wall project. A line is drawn on the center of the footing to mark the middle of the brick wall; the bricks are dry-laid, and then the first course is set in mortar. Courses are filled between leads, joints are tooled, and the wall is capped off. The only difference is in the layout of the wall on the footing and the use of a single wythe. The design specifics of a serpentine wall are explained here.

Design Specifics. Since serpentine walls depend on their shape for stability against overturning, it is important that the radius and depth of the curve be just right. A design rule of thumb based on proportional relationships can be used: The radius of the curve cannot be more than two times the wall height, and the depth from front to back must be at least one-half the wall height. The maximum height for a serpentine wall is no greater than 15 times the wall thickness.

You can build curved walls using ordinary rectangular bricks laid lengthwise in the stretcher position. If the radius of the curve is too small, though, the corners of each brick will stick out slightly and create a basket weave effect. The minimum radius required to produce a smooth curve with brick stretchers is about 8 feet.

Serpentine walls should be built on flat ground, as they do not lend themselves well to sloping terrain. Don't plan to build a wall that must be altered to curve around obstructions. It is complicated to build and requires an architect. The graceful curves and shallow recesses of a serpentine wall lend themselves to distinctive landscaping.

Leave at least 1 inch between the ends of the wall and any adjacent construction to allow for expansion of the brick. You cannot use ordinary expansion joints in a serpentine

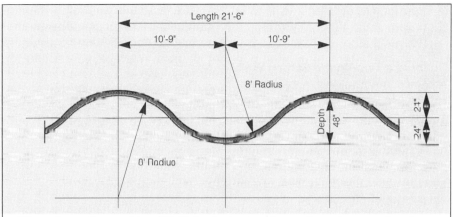

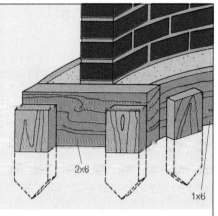

Planning a Serpentine Wall. In designing the wall, make sure that the radius of the curve is no more than two times the wall height and the depth from front to back is at least half the wall height.

Curved Footings. Bend 1x6 lumber in the gentle curves you will need for the footing.

wall because the wall depends on continuity for its stability–the wall must be free to expand over its whole length.

Planning a Serpentine Wall

Let's say you want to build a 4-foot-high serpentine wall that uses an 8-foot-radius curve and has a depth from front to back of 4 feet. (The radius is equal to twice the height, and the depth is equal to the height, so the design meets our rule-of-thumb criteria.) You can make the length whatever you want, starting and stopping at any place along the curve, but it is easiest to work from the centerline of one curve to the centerline of another. Use modular brick measuring nominally 4 by 8 inches. With an 8-foot radius and 4-foot depth, the distance from the center of one curve to the center of the next is 10 feet 9 inches. The wall is built in a running bond and is 18 courses tall.

Curved Footings. As with other types of brick walls, the serpentine single-wythe wall needs a concrete footing to support it. The footing must be wide enough to prevent overturning and deep enough to resist frost heave in the soil. A footing for this type of wall should be 6 inches thick, 12 inches wide, and follow the same curved shape as the wall. For footings that must be set very deep, it will be much more economical to

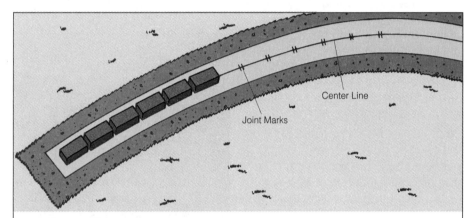

Marking the Footing. Draw a line along the center of the footing to indicate the center of the wall's single wythe. Place the first course of bricks in a dry run; then mark the joint locations.

build a concrete wall up to within a few inches of grade rather than building several courses of brick below ground level. Follow the instructions in "Concrete Footings," on page 10, for how to build concrete footings. You'll need to use 1x6 lumber for the forms as they will bend to the gentle, long curves.

Marking the Footing. When the footing has cured for a week, draw a line down the exact center of the footing. Since the footing is 12 inches wide, measure and mark 6 inches from either side at about every 3 feet, then make a line to connect the marks. This line will be used to center the wythe of bricks. As with the garden wall project, begin to lay the first course in a dry run and mark the joint locations on the footing.

Estimate the number of bricks you will need by multiplying the number of units in the wall length times the number of courses in the wall height. Estimate 14 cubic feet of mortar for every 100 square feet of wall surface. Refer to "Mortar," on page 24, to estimate individual ingredients. Now that the footing has been marked with the location of the first course, the wall is built just like any other brick wall. Simply begin from "Creating the Brick Leads," on page 35, and continue through the steps to the end of the garden wall project to build a serpentine wall. Since you can't stretch a string line along the curve, check level and plumb frequently with a 4-foot level and keep the coursing accurate with a story pole.

Brick Screen Wall

By omitting bricks to form a pattern of openings, solid brick can be used to build what are called screen walls. A screen wall provides privacy while still allowing light and air through the wall. This type of wall works well to hide a large air-conditioning unit or to shield a trash can area while still allowing ventilation. You can alternate pierced sections of wall with solid brick sections to make the wall stronger; if necessary, you can add supporting piers.

There are several different styles of brick screen wall. One of the simplest to build and most attractive consists of two rows or wythes of brick laid in the English bond pattern, shown on page 30. In this pattern, the courses of brick alternate between stretcher and header courses. When modified to create a pierced screen wall, every other header brick is omitted to form the opening pattern. The remaining headers tie the two wythes together and provide support for the stretchers. The first five courses in the illustration are laid as a solid wall to form a good base. The middle courses are then laid in the screen pattern, and the upper portion of the wall is finished with three more solid courses, then a rowlock coping.

Use a modular size brick–one that is 7⅝ inches long, 3⅝ inches wide, and 2¼ inches tall. When laid in the wall with standard ⅜-inch mortar joints, the nominal size of this brick is 8 inches long and 4 inches wide. When laid as a header, the length of the brick is the same as two stretchers with a joint between, so the header fits exactly across the width of the two-wythe wall. Three courses of bricks with mortar joints are also 8 inches high, so all of your dimensions can be planned as multiples of 4 inches, which is the nominal length of half a brick. Before doing any construction, draw a plan of the wall to scale, making each brick twice as long as it is wide. If you make the wall 7 feet 4 inches

or 8 feet long rather than 7 feet 6 inches, you will need only whole and half bricks.

Building a Two-Wythe Screen Wall.
A brick screen wall with two wythes is built with supporting pilasters every 12 feet to make the wall stronger. Small pilasters can be built for walls no higher than 4 feet; larger pilasters are used for taller walls. Alternating courses of brick in the wall must overlap the brick in the pilaster to form a strong interlocking structure. See "Adding Pilasters for Strength," on page 32, for more information. Plan to adjust the footing for the additional width of the pilasters.

To build a screen wall, follow the instructions for a brick garden wall starting on page 32 and continue to the end. When you've reached the header courses of the screened section, simply omit every other brick, leaving only the ones that will support the ends of the stretcher units in the next course. Center the headers over the joints between the stretcher units below so that they will provide about 2 inches of bed surface for each stretcher they will support in the next course. In this way, you'll create the screen pattern. Tool the mortar joints in the "voids" of the screen pattern as you would all the other bed and head joints of the wall.

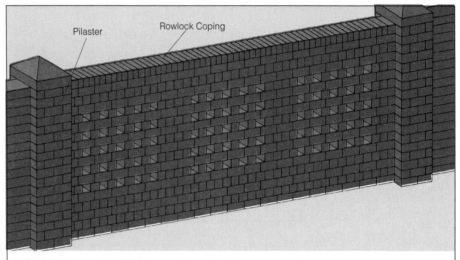

Brick Screen Wall. By omitting bricks in a regular pattern you can create a wall that blocks the view while still permitting ventilation.

Building a Two-Wythe Screen Wall. For the screened section omit every other brick in the header courses, leaving the ones that will support the ends of the stretcher units for the next course.

BUILDING BLOCK WALLS

Concrete block styles have gone way beyond the utilitarian look of gray "cinder blocks." Attractive colors and textures as well as new products such as interlocking retaining-wall blocks offer new opportunities to use this material. Block projects are simple to build, easy to start and stop at your leisure, and extremely durable.

In this chapter, you will learn how to build a basic block wall, a decorative screen block wall, and a tree well and retaining wall.

Concrete Block Garden Wall

Like any mortared masonry wall, a block garden wall requires a footing. To learn how to build a proper footing for your wall see "Concrete Footings" page 10.

Depending on its length and whether it abuts another structure, your block wall may require control joints. In addition, all block walls require steel reinforcement. Before beginning the step-by-step process of constructing the wall, this section will discuss how you can meet control joint and reinforcement requirements.

Control Joints for Concrete Block

Concrete masonry will crack when it loses residual manufacturing and construction moisture and shrinks. This is unavoidable. Control joints are continuous vertical joints purposely made weaker than the rest of the joints so that the cracking will occur in straight lines rather than randomly. Because of the way they are formed, these joints maintain a wall's lateral strength. To make the control joints continuous, you'll need to interrupt the running bond with half blocks, as shown.

Cracking is likely to occur at changes of height in the wall (such as with a stepped footing) or the thickness of the wall (such as at a pilaster). Usually, you'll place control joints where the wall abuts other structures and at a spacing of two and a half times the wall height for joint reinforcement located in every third bed joint or three times the wall height for joint reinforcement located in every second bed joint. Control joints are created by using tongue-and-groove blocks, placing a Michigan joint, or using a premolded joint material.

Tongue-and-Groove Blocks. These blocks are specially shaped units that fit together without any mortar. Their matched design holds the wall laterally but allows for shrinkage.

Plan for the use of these blocks when designing the wall and ordering materials.

Michigan Joint. This is a control joint between two ordinary flanged concrete blocks. A strip of building paper is folded on one side of the joint and the hollow core is filled with mortar. The building paper allows the mortar to bond to only one side. The mortar creates a plug that provides lateral strength. This type of joint may require cutting more blocks.

Premolded Control Joints. Use rubber inserts shaped like a plus sign (+). They fit into grooves formed in specially made blocks. Again, plan the use of these blocks when designing the wall and ordering materials.

Control joints in concrete block walls must be sealed against moisture. To do this, caulk the edges with a silicone sealant. Be sure to place closed-cell backer rod (available from masonry suppliers) behind the sealant to maintain the right depth for the sealant.

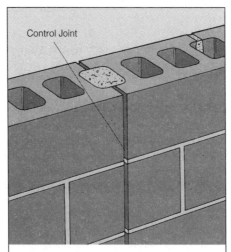

Control Joint

Control Joints for Concrete Block. Concrete blocks will crack and require continuous control joints to control where the crack will occur.

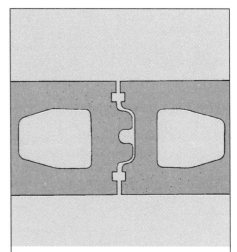

Tongue-and-Groove Blocks. These blocks fit together without mortar, providing lateral support while allowing the wall to shrink.

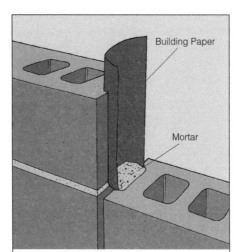

Building Paper

Mortar

Michigan Joint. In this joint, a piece of roofing felt prevents a bond between joints while allowing mortar to bond to one block.

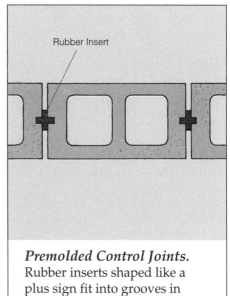

Rubber Insert

Premolded Control Joints. Rubber inserts shaped like a plus sign fit into grooves in premolded blocks.

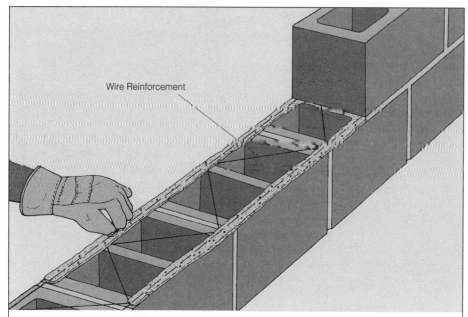

Joint Reinforcement. Use wire joint reinforcement to minimize shrinkage cracking in block walls.

Joint Reinforcement

Every block wall should have steel joint reinforcement to minimize shrinkage cracking. Beginning with the second course, spread mortar only on the edges of the blocks. Place wire joint reinforcement between the first and second course and in every second or third bed joint after that.

Installing joint reinforcement can be awkward. When mortar is spread the length of two or three blocks, as is customary, only part of the length of the joint reinforcement can be embedded. The remainder rests on dry block and must be embedded as subsequent blocks are laid by laying mortar on top and jiggling the wire to get mortar to flow under it. Where joint reinforcement must be overlapped to splice two sections, nest the wires together in the joint, overlapping them about 16 inches.

The width of the joint reinforcement should be about 1 inch less than the width of the blocks—so that it is protected by a good cover of mortar on both sides of the wall. Joint reinforcement must stop on either side of a control joint. It cannot continue through it.

Locating the Wall on the Footing

Design the wall on a piece of graph paper using one square to represent an 8x16-inch block. Take into account the use of control joints and reinforcement in your design. Begin to build the wall following these steps.

1 Marking the Wall Location. After your concrete footing has cured for at least seven days, brush all debris from the top surface. Measure and mark the location of the outside face of the wall, being careful to center the masonry in the middle of the footing. As with the footing, batter boards and string are used to determine the corner locations. Square your corners and snap a chalk line along the length of the footing, locating the wall. To ensure that the corners are square, use the 3-4-5 triangle method. From the outside corner point, measure up 4 feet along one leg of the footing and 3 feet along the other leg. The two lines are square when the diagonal between the two points measures 5 feet. To square the line of a wall against an existing wall, use a carpenter's square against the line and the wall.

2 Cutting Half Blocks. The wall construction is easiest using only whole and half blocks. Cut half-size blocks now, as needed for the ends, with either a brickset or a circular saw with a masonry cutting blade. To use a brickset, place the block on sand or loose soil. With a

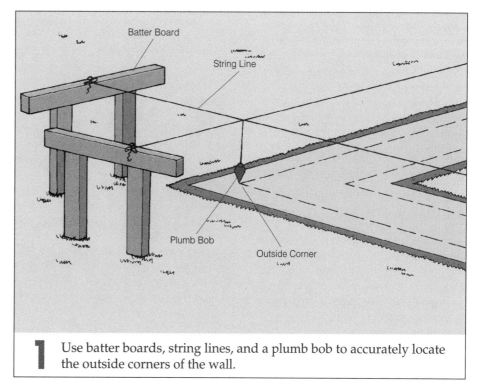

1 Use batter boards, string lines, and a plumb bob to accurately locate the outside corners of the wall.

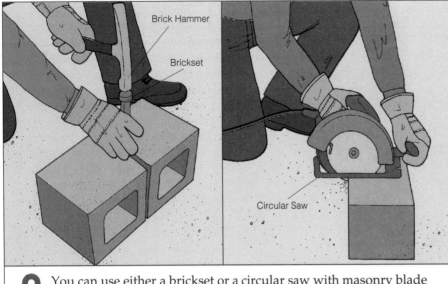

Brick Hammer

Brickset

Circular Saw

2 You can use either a brickset or a circular saw with masonry blade to make half blocks.

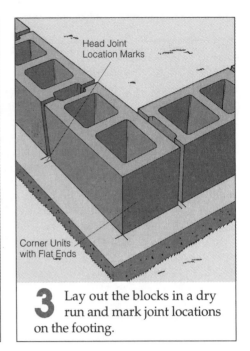

Head Joint Location Marks

Corner Units with Flat Ends

3 Lay out the blocks in a dry run and mark joint locations on the footing.

hammer, strike the brickset to mark the cut on both faces of the block. Then work along the line again, striking harder until the block breaks. Always wear protective eyewear when cutting blocks. With the saw, just set the depth equal to the flange width and cut the block.

3 **Dry-Laying the Block.** Check the wall length by laying out a dry course of block. Start at the corners and work from both ends toward the middle. Use a piece of ⅜-inch plywood to space the units. Adjust the size of the joints between the ends of the units (called head joints) to take up slight variations in the size of the blocks. Using a marker, pencil, or chalk, make long slash marks on the footing at the head joints so that you will be able to confirm the spacing of the first course as you work.

Building the Wall Leads

Begin wall construction by building leading sections, or leads, at the ends or corners. Masonry walls are always laid from the outside ends or corners toward the middle, which helps establish the correct spacing and coursing heights for the rest of the wall. The first course of a corner or end lead for a block wall should

be three units long. The second and successive courses are set back one-half block in each course. This establishes a running bond pattern in which the units of one course are offset one-half block from the courses above and below.

1 **Laying the First Block.** Mix a batch of mortar and begin the first course of the lead at one end of the wall. Pick up a trowel full of

mortar and spread it along the chalk line marking the wall's outer face. Use enough mortar to make a bed that is ½ to ¾ inch thick, slightly wider than a block, and about three blocks long. Don't skimp on the mortar or you'll wind up with voids under the blocks, which will substantially weaken the bond. Lay the corner or end unit first, pressing it firmly down into the mortar. Measure to make sure the resulting mortar bed is about

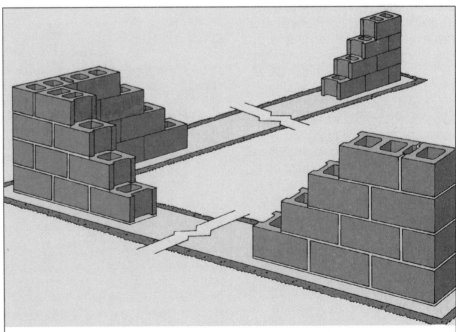

Building the Wall Leads. You will begin construction by building the corner leads, and then you'll work in toward the middle.

⅜ inch high; tap the unit lightly with the trowel handle if necessary. You can correct slight irregularities in the concrete footing by varying the thickness of the first mortar bed, up to a maximum of about ¾ inch, to keep the block course level. Use a 4-foot level to check that the block is both level and plumb. This is the most important block of the wall.

2 Buttering the Block Flanges.

Butter the head joints of concrete block by standing the units on end and swiping mortar onto the flanges with the edge of the trowel. When you set the block, place the wider ends of the flanges up to hold more mortar. Lift the block by the ends and place it gently on the mortar bed and firmly against the adjacent block. Mortar should squeeze from both the head and bed joints. Remove the excess mortar from the face of the blocks with the trowel blade. In this way, lay the three blocks for the first course of the lead section and check for level and plumb.

3 Mortaring the Face Shells.

While the first course of a concrete block wall is laid in a full mortar bed, the rest of the wall is laid with what is called face-shell bedding. The 8x16-inch outside surfaces of a concrete block are called the face shells. Mortar is placed along the top of the face shells, which is about 1½ inches wide. Place the mortar with a downward swiping motion of the trowel. This is more difficult than laying mortar beds for brick because the bed is narrower. Mortaring block will take some practice.

Spread mortar for the next bed joint on top of the face shells of the three blocks in the first course. If your wall has joint reinforcement between the first and second courses, install it now. See "Joint Reinforcement," on page 47.

The second course will start with a half block to establish the running bond. The second course of a corner can be a whole block. Butter the

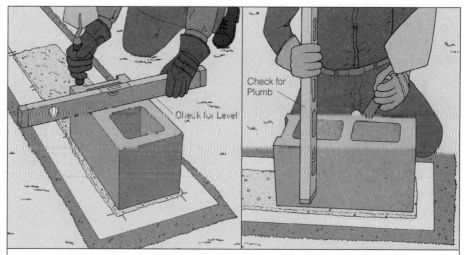

1 Take special care to get the first block properly positioned and perfectly level and plumb.

2 Swipe mortar on the flanges of one side of a block and set it gently into place.

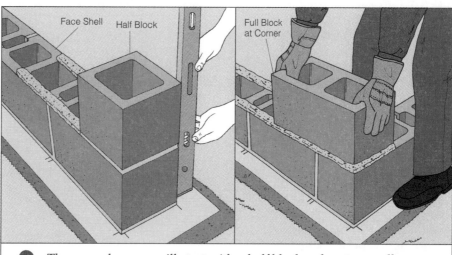

3 The second course will start with a half block unless two walls are meeting at a corner.

4 Check the "rack" of the leads with a level or straight 2x4.

flanges of each block in the second course before it is laid. Set the blocks firmly into the mortar bed and against the adjacent units. Mortar should squeeze out of both the bed and head joints.

4 **Finishing the Leads.** Lay the rest of the leads, setting the blocks back one-half unit in each course of the end leads to establish the running bond pattern. Scrape excess mortar off the blocks with the trowel's edge. A 4-foot level or straight 2x4 laid carefully along the "rack" of the lead should touch the corner of each block when placed on the flanges, and should be perfectly level when placed on the sides of the block. Use a story pole to set the vertical coursing as you build your leads. Build the leads four courses high.

Building Up the Block Wall

As with any masonry unit project, the wall is built by filling in between leads and then starting over with new leads built higher and higher. Here's how to complete the wall:

1 **Preparing a String Line.** To fill in the masonry between leads, stretch a line to mark the top of each course as you build up the wall. Use line blocks and mason's twine to do this. (Mason's twine is better than

cotton string because it will stretch tightly without breaking.) Prepare the line blocks as explained in "Preparing Line Blocks," page 38. Hook one line block on the corner of the lead so that the line is level with the top of the block in the course you're working on. Stretch the line to the opposite corner lead and hook the other line block at the same height. Check the line with a line level. The line blocks hold the string about 1⁄16 inch away from the face of the wall. The masonry between the leads can now be "laid to the line" to keep the wall straight and the block course level.

2 **Filling in the First Course.** Fill in the first course between leads, buttering the flanges as you lay blocks in the mortar on the footing. Check the face of the units to make sure they are correctly laid along the

chalk line and have the proper head joint thickness. As you work, continually check the tops of the blocks with a 4-foot level to make sure that each course is level. Tap down any units that are set too high. Remove units that are set too low, cut away the mortar, and lay the unit with fresh mortar. Check the blocks with a level to make sure they are plumb; use the side of the level as a straightedge to align the face of the units in each course. Any unit that is dislodged after it is initially set must be removed, the mortar cut away, and the unit laid with fresh mortar. It is crucial that the first course of block be level and plumb because it is the base for the entire wall. You can allow for slight variations in block length by adjusting the thickness of the head joints between the ends of the units, but try to keep the head joints uniform.

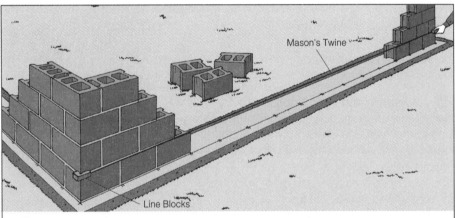

1 Use line blocks and mason's twine to delineate the face of the wall. This will help keep the wall level and plumb.

2 Fill in the blocks between the leads. Check frequently that the blocks are plumb and level.

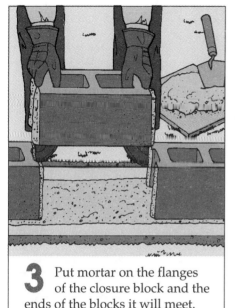

3 Put mortar on the flanges of the closure block and the ends of the blocks it will meet.

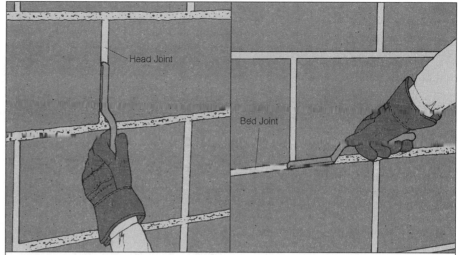

Head Joint

Bed Joint

4 Use a rounded tool to make concave joints, doing the head joints first and then the bed joints.

3 **Laying the Closure Block.** The last block to be put into place in a course is called the closure block. You should have just enough space left for this block plus a head joint on each end. To make sure you get full head joints, butter the ends of the adjacent blocks and both ends of the closure block. Lower the block into place from above, being careful not to dislodge the adjacent blocks.

4 **Tooling the Mortar Joints.** As you lay the concrete blocks, remove excess mortar from the face of the joints with the edge of the trowel blade. After the mortar has begun to cure, however, the surfaces of the head and bed joints need to be tooled to compress the mortar and decrease moisture absorption at the surface. It is important that joints be tooled at a consistent moisture content so that they do not appear light in some areas and dark in others. The joints are ready for tooling when the mortar is "thumbprint" hard, meaning that you can press your thumb against the mortar and leave a print impression without mortar sticking to your thumb.

Use a rounded jointing tool to make concave joints. Tool the head joints first and then the bed joints. Do not wait until you have finished a large section of wall before you tool the

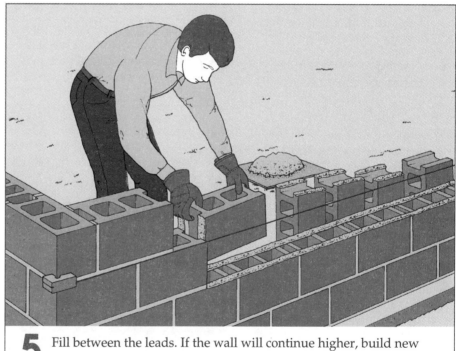

5 Fill between the leads. If the wall will continue higher, build new corner leads.

joints. Check the mortar frequently, and tool the joints a few at a time when the surface is just the right consistency. As the joints are tooled, small pieces of mortar, called tailings, will be squeezed out at the edges of the joints. Remove them with the edge of the trowel.

5 **Filling between the Leads.** After laying the closure block and confirming the first course is

level and plumb, the wall can be built up rapidly. Simply continue the process of buttering the flanges of each block as you lay it and placing it on the previous course on which a face-shell bed of mortar has been spread.

When you get comfortable with the block-laying process, you can set three or four blocks on end, mortar their flanges, mortar the bed joint, and lay a number of the blocks in rapid succession. Just be sure to never disturb the line blocks and to check for level and plumb often. Scrape off any excess mortar.

When you have filled in the courses between your leads, build up the ends or corners of the walls again to form new leads. Repeat the process of filling in courses and building leads until you reach the next-to-last course of block below the coping.

Finishing the Top of the Wall

The top of a concrete block wall requires a coping to protect the wall joints from water penetration. A coping is particularly important in cold climates with a lot of rain or snow. When water trapped in a wall freezes, it expands and can cause serious damage to the block and mortar.

1 Placing the Wire Netting.
Before the coping is added, the cores of the top course of block are filled with mortar. To prevent this mortar from falling into the wall below, lay strips of wire netting in the bed joint below the top course of block. Cut the wire netting about ¼ inch short of the edge of the face-shell. Nestle the wire netting in the middle of the mortar. Lay the top course of block as described above.

2 Filling the Block Cores with Mortar. Fill the cores of the top course of block with mortar. Mix a batch of mortar with a little more water than usual so it will pour into the cores easily. Fill all of the hollow cores as well as any spaces between blocks. Stir the mortar in the cores a little to get rid of air bubbles. If the mortar settles, add more to bring it flush with the top surface of the block.

3 Laying the Coping. Before installing the coping, install flashing as described in "Installing Flashing" on page 40. Cap the wall with flat coping block or with pieces of flat stone. Make sure the joints between coping units are

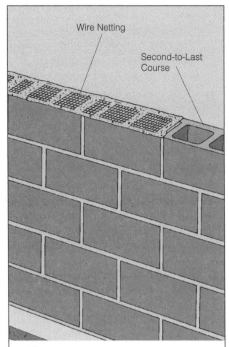

1 To prevent the mortar from falling farther into the wall, place wire netting on top of the second-to-last course.

2 Mix a loose batch of mortar and use a coffee can to fill the last course's cores.

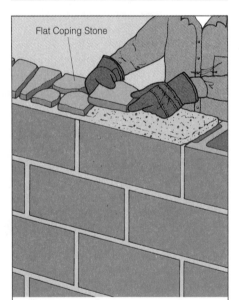

3 Use flat coping block or pieces of flat stone for coping. Fill the joints thoroughly and tool them.

4 Use a small chunk of concrete block to scrape residue off the wall.

completely full, then tool them to compress the surface of the mortar as described previously.

4 Cleaning the Wall. Remove mortar splatters with the trowel when they are almost dry, then rub

the wall with a small piece of concrete block to remove any residue. **Caution:** *Do not use muriatic acid on concrete masonry because it will dissolve the cement in the block face, etching the surface.*

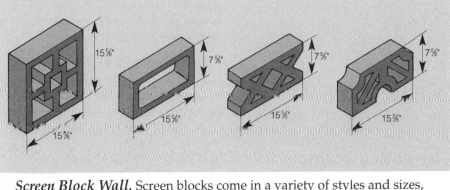

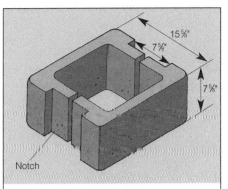

Screen Block Wall. Screen blocks come in a variety of styles and sizes, although most are designed to work with an 8x16-in. building module, including joints.

Screen Wall Piers. Pier blocks have two parts. When assembled, they form notches that fit around the screen blocks.

Screen Block Wall

Decorative concrete block screen walls create a wall with a pattern of openings that provide both privacy and ventilation. There are more sizes and shapes of decorative screen blocks than can be mentioned here. However, the most common size of concrete block has actual face dimensions of 7⅝ by 15⅝ inches. When laid with standard ⅜-inch mortar joints, the nominal face dimensions for each unit module are 8 x 16 inches. The face dimensions of some screen blocks are (nominally) 12 inches square or 16 inches square. Screen blocks come in thicknesses of 4, 6, or 8 inches. Choose a style of block that you like and that is readily available in your area; then plan the length and height of a wall to be a multiple of the block length so that you will use only whole units.

Screen Wall Pilasters. Block screen walls are usually built with supporting pilasters for added strength. A pilaster is a column of masonry that is built as part of a wall. One of the simplest ways to build pilasters is to use special pilaster blocks. These units have notches, into which the screen block can be nestled, and a center core for reinforcing steel embedded in mortar.

The distance between pilasters is proportional to the nominal wall thickness. As a rule, a 4-inch-thick wall has pilasters every 6 feet, a

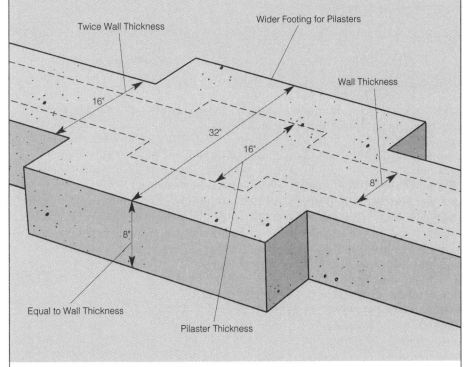

Screen Wall Footings. The thickness of the footing is the same as the thickness of the wall, while the width of the footing is twice the thickness of the wall.

6-inch-thick wall has pilasters every 9 feet, and an 8-inch-thick wall has pilasters every 12 feet.

On a piece of graph paper, draw an elevation (side view) of your wall, and use it to calculate the number of screen block and pilaster units you will need. Since the pilaster blocks are made in halves, remember to double the number of units shown in the elevation to account for both sides of the wall.

Screen Wall Footings. Once you have drawn your wall plan, you can design a concrete footing to support the wall. The footing must be wide enough to prevent overturning and deep enough to resist frost heave in the soil. The thickness of the footing is the same as the thickness of the wall. The width of the footing is twice the thickness of the wall. For example, if the screen block is 8 inches thick, the footing is 8 inches thick

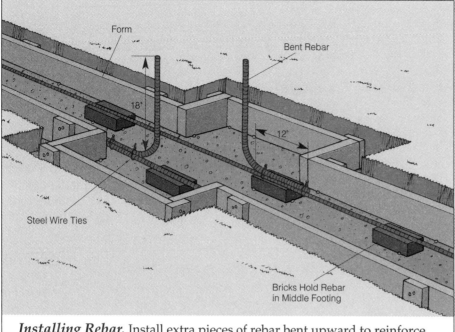

Installing Rebar. Install extra pieces of rebar bent upward to reinforce the piers.

Labels in figure: Form; Bent Rebar; 18"; 12"; Steel Wire Ties; Bricks Hold Rebar in Middle Footing

and 16 inches wide. At the pilasters, the footing must be wider. For a nominal 16x16-inch pilaster, widen the footing to a 32-inch square.

Installing Rebar. Place two extra ⅜-inch steel reinforcing bars in the concrete footing and bend them upward to fit inside the pilaster block. Rebar can be ordered from the supplier, bent to any angle. You may also be able to rent a tool that bends rebar. (The tool is similar to a hickey used to bend electrical conduit.) These rebar "dowels" must be long enough to stick out the top of the footing by at least 18 inches. Make the horizontal leg of the rebar dowels at least 12 inches long, and tie them with steel wire to the rebar in the footing. Rebar can be cut with a reciprocating saw.

Calculate and measure the spacing of the dowels carefully so that the rebar will align properly within the pilaster cavity. If necessary, lay out a dry course of block on the ground next to the footing forms before you pour concrete in them. Read "Concrete Footings," on page 10, and build a footing as directed.

Building the Screen Wall

The following project shows how to build a straight length of screen wall. The project has five courses of 16-inch-square screen block. Although not shown here, you can build a screen wall with corners. Corners are made with pilaster units shaped to accept screen blocks

at a 90-degree angle. Ask your building supply dealer about the availability of such blocks.

1 Snapping a Chalk Line. After your concrete footing has cured properly, brush off the top surface. Measure and mark the location of the outside face of the wall, being careful to center the masonry in the middle of the footing. Snap a chalk line along the length of the footing. (If you have corners in the wall, follow the instructions in "Locating and Excavating" on page 10, before snapping the lines.)

2 Dry-Laying the Screen Blocks. With no mortar, set a whole pilaster block on the footing with the rebar in the center, and check the wall length by laying out a dry course of screen block. The wall is built by starting at the pilasters and working the blocks from both ends toward the middle. Use a piece of ⅜-inch plywood to space the units. Adjust the size of the joints between the ends of the blocks to take up slight variations in the size of the block. Using a marker, pencil, or chalk, make long slash marks at the head joints to confirm the spacing of the

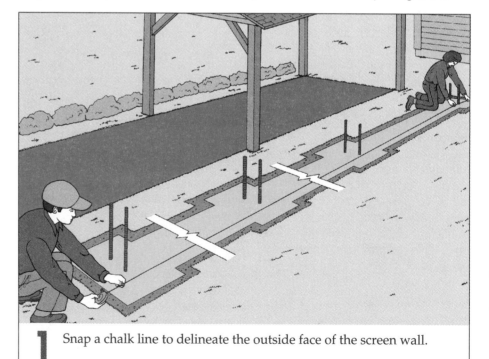

1 Snap a chalk line to delineate the outside face of the screen wall.

first course as you work. Remove the pilaster and screen blocks.

3 Setting Rebar for the Pilasters.

After laying out the dry run and marking chalk lines on the footing, you are ready to begin building the pilasters. The reinforced pilasters are built as hollow shells around the reinforcing steel and then mortared solid. Mix a batch of mortar with a little more water than usual to pour in the pilasters. Before building the pilasters, attach a length of #3 rebar (⅜ inch in diameter) onto the dowels that were left protruding from the footing. Cut the rebar with a reciprocating saw so that it will extend 2 inches below the top of the last course of pilaster blocks. Overlap the rebar and dowel at least 12 inches and tie them together tightly with steel wire. The steel in the pilaster must be held upright until it is embedded in mortar.

4 Laying the Pilaster Blocks.

Build the pilasters before you begin laying the screen block. Place mortar on the horizontal surface of the footing to form bed joints and on the head joints between the front and back block; then set the blocks firmly into the mortar and against one another. Hold a 4-foot level on the side of the blocks to confirm plumb, and check the top for level. Build four courses of pilaster blocks (32 inches high), and stop.

Clean excess mortar off the blocks with the edge of the trowel. Tool the joints when they're "thumbprint" hard. See "Tooling Mortar Joints," page 38.

5 Mortaring the Pilasters.

After building four courses, allow the mortar to cure overnight. Then fill the cavity solidly with a mortar mix to which extra water has been added. Stop each pour about 1 inch below the top of the fourth course. This will form a "key" with the next pour and make the pilaster stronger. Use a length of rebar to stir the mortar slightly to make sure that all the corners and recesses are filled and that there are no pockets of trapped air. Let it cure for a week before building the next four courses of the pilaster. While you're waiting, fill in the screen blocks between the pilasters.

6 Preparing Control Joints.

Control joints are continuous, weakened joints designed to accommodate the natural shrinkage of concrete masonry in such a way that cracking will occur at these joints rather than at random locations. To make a control joint in this project, line one side of the pilaster block with

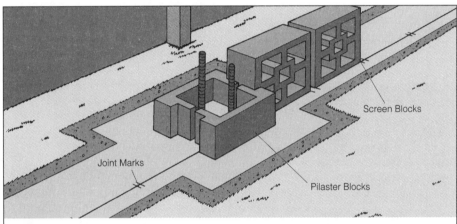

2 Lay out the first course of blocks, including the piers, to see how they fit on the foundation. You may have to adjust the mortar joint size slightly to make the blocks fit. Mark the joint locations on the footing.

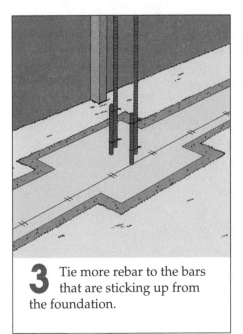

3 Tie more rebar to the bars that are sticking up from the foundation.

4 Build the piers to their full height before laying the screen block.

5 After every four courses, allow the piers to set overnight. Then fill them with mortar before continuing.

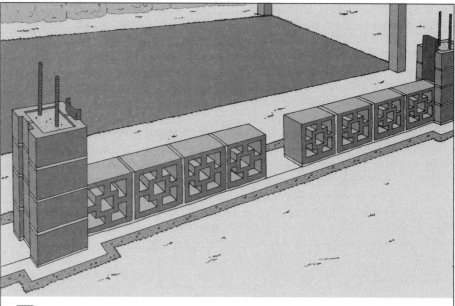

6 Use roofing felt to create control joints between the piers and screen blocks.

7 Lay the first course of screen blocks, beginning at the piers and working toward the middle.

roofing felt or building paper before mortaring in the screen block. Locate a control joint on one side of each pilaster. Before going any further, read "Preparing Line Blocks," on page 38, and set a line for the first course of screen blocks.

7 Laying the First Course of Screen Block. Mix a batch of mortar and begin to lay the first course of screen block. Spread mortar along the chalk line on the footing and on the side of the screen block that will be nestled in the pilaster. Begin at the pilasters and work toward the middle. It is important that this first block course be level–correct slight irregularities in the concrete footing by varying the thickness of the first mortar bed. Use a 4-foot level to check that the block is both level and plumb and that the faces are aligned to the mason's twine.

Mortar the entire side of the screen block for the head joints and maintain a ⅜-inch joint size. Remove excess mortar at the face of the units with the edge of a trowel.

8 Filling in the First Course. The last unit to be put into place in a course is called the closure

8 To make sure you fill the closure block head joints with mortar, put mortar both on the sides of the closure block and the sides of the adjoining blocks.

Head Joint

Bed Joints

block. You should have just enough space left for this block plus a head joint on each side. To make sure you get full head joints, spread mortar on the ends of the adjacent block and on both ends of the closure block. Lower the block into place from above, being careful not to dislodge

the adjacent blocks. See "Tooling Mortar Joints," page 38.

9 Installing Joint Reinforcement. Screen walls require reinforcement in every bed joint. Spread mortar on the top of the screen blocks, and place wire joint rein-

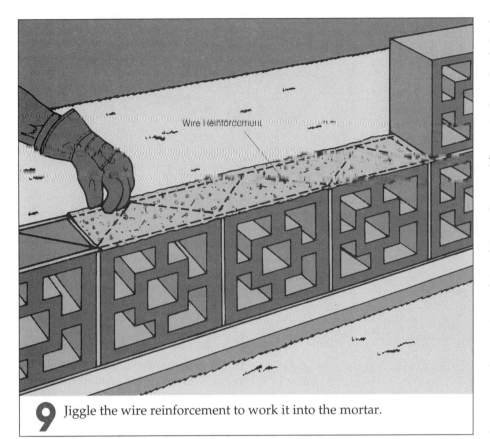

9 Jiggle the wire reinforcement to work it into the mortar.

forcement in the first bed joint. This can be awkward: If mortar is spread the length of two or three blocks as is customary, only part of the length of joint reinforcement can be embedded. The remainder rests on dry block and must be embedded by spreading mortar on top and jiggling the wire to get mortar to flow under it.

If joint reinforcement must be overlapped to splice two sections, nest the wires together in the joint and overlap them about 16 inches. The width of the joint reinforcement should be about 1 inch less than the actual width of the units so that it will be protected by a good cover of mortar on both sides of the wall. Stop joint reinforcement on either side of control joints—do not continue it across the joint.

10 **Continuing to Build Pilasters and Lay Courses.**
As with all masonry-unit projects, the

10 When four courses are completed, build another four courses of pier, let them cure, fill the piers, and build up the screen just as you did for the first four courses.

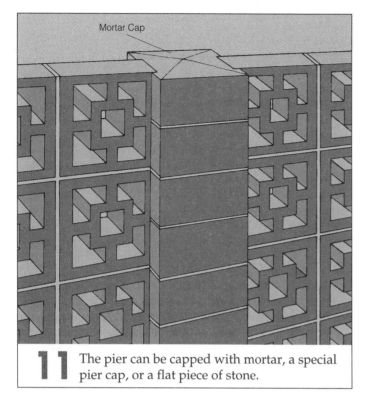

Mortar Cap

11 The pier can be capped with mortar, a special pier cap, or a flat piece of stone.

12 Remove splatters with a trowel and then rub off the residue with a scrap of concrete block.

building process for the screen wall is simply an exercise in repetition. Continue to build the pilasters, fill them to an inch from the top and then fill in the screen block courses. Lay reinforcement in each bed joint, and tool the joints as you progress. Continue until you've reached final height as per your design.

11 Capping the Pilaster. Cap the top of the pilaster with a bed of smoothly troweled mortar. Slope the mortar from a centerpoint downward to shed rain and snow. You may choose to buy a piece of flat stone and mortar it to the top of the pilaster for a decorative look. A specially molded concrete pilaster top is another option to consider.

12 Cleaning the Wall. Remove mortar splatters with the trowel when the splatters are almost dry, then rub the area with a small piece of block to remove the residue. Do not use muriatic acid on concrete masonry because it will dissolve the cement in the block face, etching the surface.

Interlocking Concrete Block

Interlocking concrete blocks are a system of mortarless masonry units that have become popular in recent years. The construction process couldn't be simpler, and there are many uses for this type of concrete block. The units lock together to form retaining walls. These walls can stabilize an earth embankment and halt erosion; create terraces in a sloping yard; form a tree well; provide raised planting beds; and serve many other landscaping

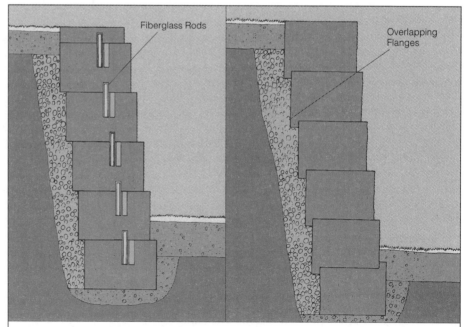

Fiberglass Rods

Overlapping Flanges

Interlocking Concrete Blocks. Some interlocking systems use fiberglass rods, others use overlapping flanges.

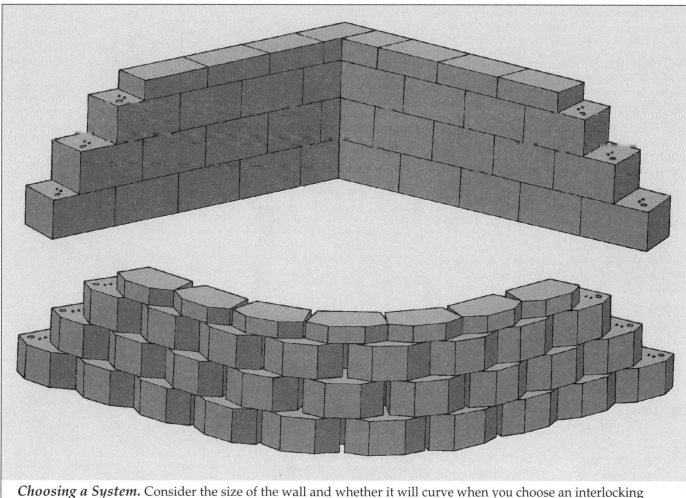

Choosing a System. Consider the size of the wall and whether it will curve when you choose an interlocking block system.

applications. Sold under a number of different trade names, the systems are available through concrete block manufacturers, masonry distributors, and building materials distributors throughout the country.

While no mortar is required for interlocking systems, some include fiberglass rods or pins to hold the individual units together, while others have flanges that overlap. The units usually have a rough, stone-like texture and are made in colors ranging from gray to buff or earth tones. Check in your area to see which system or systems are available.

Choosing a System. When choosing a system, first determine the height and length of wall you want to build. Each brand of wall system will have a different size unit, so you should

consult your supplier to determine the total number of units required. Some systems can be laid in curved lines, but others are limited to straight walls and 90-degree corners.

Terracing. With most systems, you can build a retaining wall up to 36 inches high without the need for reinforcing or special soil-retention accessories. For higher walls, systems may have special components to increase the strength of the wall and allow for drainage. As an alternative to a single high wall, consider two shorter walls stepped back against the slope.

Building a Tree Well

The following project has been designed using a kind of interlocking block that uses fiberglass pins for reinforcement. The step-by-step

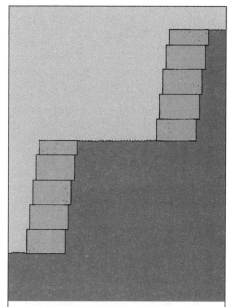

Terracing. Most interlocking systems can be built to about 36 in. high. To build higher build two walls with a terrace between.

instructions illustrate the process of building a retaining wall to create a tree well, but because the design of interlocking concrete blocks differs among manufacturers, the block you buy may have different construction criteria. Every brand of interlocking block will come with manufacturer's specifications regarding height limitations, loading strength, and base requirements. Read these specifications carefully before building.

Protecting the Tree. When building a tree well, it is important to set the wall far enough away from the tree so that you won't damage the root system when you are digging the footing, and the roots won't undermine the footing once the wall is in place. For most trees, the diameter of the root system equals the spread of the limbs, so lay out a wall that is outside the reach of the limbs.

Designing the Well. In this project, you'll build a 36-inch-high semicircular tree well using interlocking concrete units that measure 4 inches high and 12 inches square. The total wall length is 30 feet, including a 12-foot straight section and a curve with an 18-foot arc length. The 18-foot arc length is half the circumference of the circle defined by the tree's limbs. Circumference of a circle is found by multiplying the diameter by π (3.14). Divide this number by two to get half the circumference.

The 36-inch wall height requires nine courses of units (9x4 inches = 36 inches), and the 12-inch blocks make each course 30 units long. With this system, you'll also need one course of blocks below grade. Figuring ten courses times 30 units per course, the wall will require 300 units. At about 30 pounds each, these units are fairly light in weight but still heavy enough to make a hard day's labor for those unaccustomed to lifting. Be sure to lift with your legs to avoid a painful back injury or unnecessary strains.

1 **Excavating the Embankment.** As shown in the illustration,

Protecting the Tree. For most trees, the roots cover about the same diameter as the limbs. So avoid the roots by building the tree well outside the reach of the limbs.

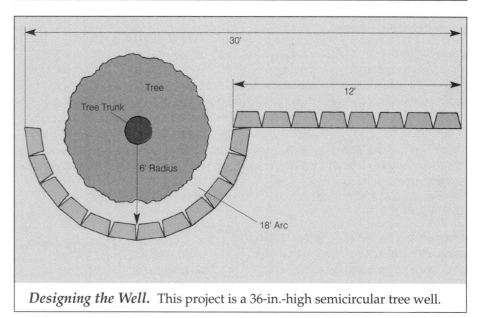

Designing the Well. This project is a 36-in.-high semicircular tree well.

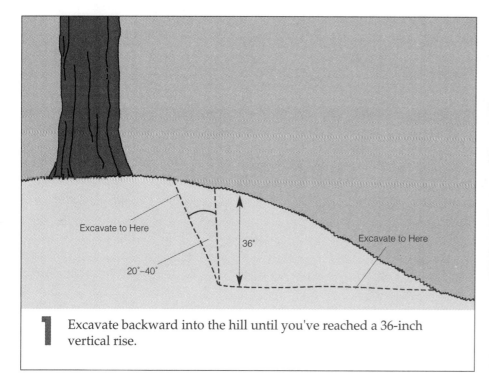

1 Excavate backward into the hill until you've reached a 36-inch vertical rise.

Excavate to Here

36"

20°–40°

Excavate to Here

2 For well-drained soils, excavate a trench to the depth of one course of blocks.

excavate backward into the hill until you've reached a 36-inch vertical rise. Continue excavating until the vertical embankment falls away at an angle of 20 to 40 degrees from 90 degrees to allow for any soil that may fall forward. Make sure you cut the embankment to make a flat base on which the units can sit and to allow placement of the required gravel backfill.

2 **Excavating the Trench.** Some interlocking block systems have the first course level to the grade; however, as mentioned before, this 36-inch-high wall will have one course of block below grade. In well-drained areas, excavate a trench along the length of the embankment 6 inches deep (4-inch-thick block plus 2 inches of sand) and 24 inches wide (12-inch-wide block plus 12 inches of gravel backfill). Remove all grass, sod, roots, and large rocks, and tamp to make the bottom of the trench level and firmly packed. Place landscape fabric in the trench and on the vertical face of the embankment. Lay the fabric over the top of the embankment by 6 inches and overlap sections by at least 6 inches. Place a 2-inch bed of sand on the fabric. The sand aids in leveling the units. Smooth

Gravel

3 For soils that drain poorly, excavate deep enough to put 4 inches of gravel or stone under the wall.

the top of the sand with a piece of 2x4, and use a level to make sure the surface is flat.

3 **Adding a Drainage Bed if Needed.** In dense soils, or soils with high clay content, or in areas with poor drainage, excavate the

trench 10 inches to place 4 inches of ⅜- to ¾-inch compactable gravel or crushed stone on the earth. This will create a drainage bed below the wall. Level the gravel drainage bed with a rake and tamp to compact it. Place a layer of landscape fabric over the gravel, then add 2 inches

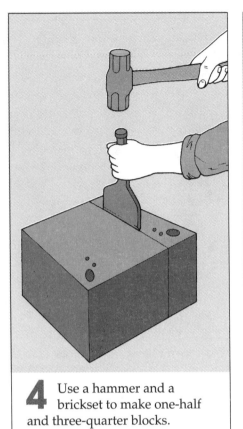

4 Use a hammer and a brickset to make one-half and three-quarter blocks.

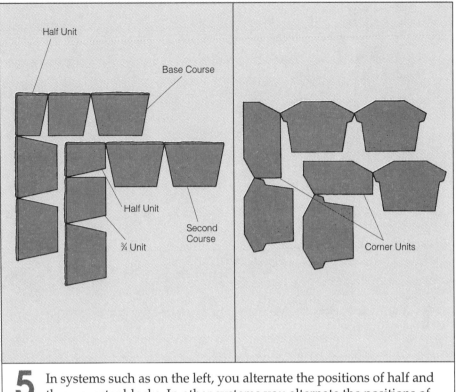

Half Unit

Base Course

Half Unit

¾ Unit

Second Course

Corner Units

5 In systems such as on the left, you alternate the positions of half and three-quarter blocks. In other systems you alternate the positions of corner units.

of sand as in Step 2 above. Use this gravel bed only if your soil has high moisture levels—it makes leveling the wall more difficult. Check with your local building department as to the base needed.

4 **Splitting Units for Corner.**
Some systems may come with specially shaped blocks, making cutting corner units unnecessary. If not, split half- and three-quarter units for the corners using a hammer and brickset. First score the unit all the way around, then break it with a few sharp blows. To avoid eye injury, be sure to wear safety glasses when splitting blocks.

5 **Setting Base Course Corner.**
Starting at the 90-degree corner between the straight and curved wall sections, lay the first course of units, butting each unit snugly against the next. To form the corner, you'll alternate the half- and three-quarter units in each course. Follow the directions for using a manufacturer's prefabricated corner unit.

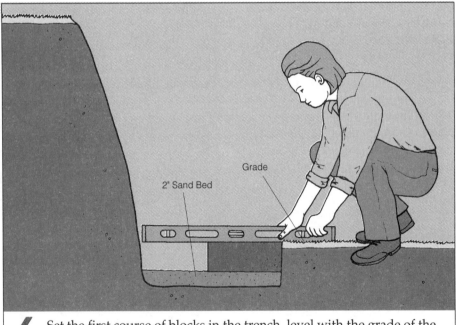

Grade

2" Sand Bed

6 Set the first course of blocks in the trench, level with the grade of the tree well excavation.

Set only the first course now. In some systems, subsequent corner courses are bonded to the course above and below with a masonry adhesive as recommended by the block manufacturer.

6 **Laying the First Course.** For this sample project, the first course of blocks must be set with their tops level to the grade. Level each unit on its own (back to front and side to side) and to adjacent units. Use the sand bed to correct minor irregularities in leveling by tapping the block down into the bed or building up the bed slightly. It is imperative that the base course be level, or the wall will not be stable. Complete the entire first course before starting the second course. Do not align the course according to the rough faces of the blocks, instead align the pinholes or the machine-smooth backs of the blocks.

7 Filling any Voids and Backfill. Shovel ⅜- to ¾-inch compactable gravel or crushed stone behind the first course of units and between the blocks in the curved section to secure them in place and to provide drainage for soil moisture. Some blocks have voids in them that must be filled with gravel. Tamp the gravel behind the wall. Gravel backfill is added after each course.

8 Setting the Second Course. First clean off any excess backfill material from the tops of the first course of units. Set the second course of units on top of the first, offsetting each unit one-half the length of the block below to form a running-bond pattern. To secure the units to one another, insert the fiberglass pins in the holes on the top of the base course and lower a block onto the pins of two adjacent blocks.

Interlocking blocks may be set in a near vertical position or sloped back into an embankment. The backward slope of the wall is dictated by the pin placement in the blocks. There are usually two or more pin holes on each side of the block. By placing the pins in the back holes every course or every other course (as suggested by the manufacturer), the wall will slope backward. Some other types of retaining wall systems align the blocks with a lip on the back of the unit, or other means.

9 Setting the Remaining Courses. Set the remaining

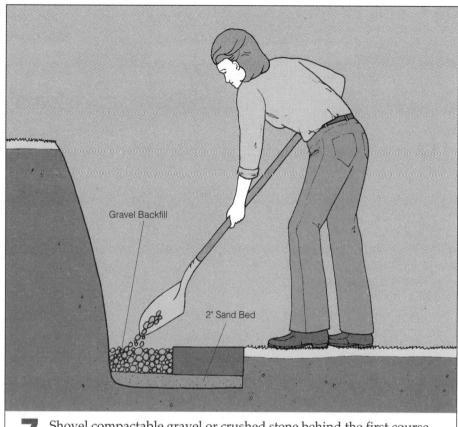

Gravel Backfill

2" Sand Bed

7 Shovel compactable gravel or crushed stone behind the first course of block and between blocks in the curved section.

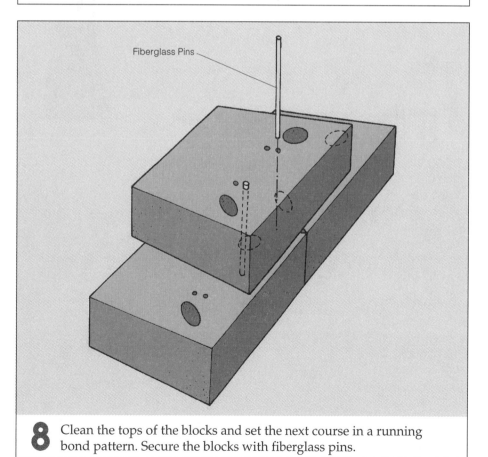

Fiberglass Pins

8 Clean the tops of the blocks and set the next course in a running bond pattern. Secure the blocks with fiberglass pins.

courses in the same manner as the first and second. Alternate the half- and three-quarter units in each course at the corner, insert the locking pins, and place the gravel backfill until you reach the 36-inch wall height.

10 **Capping the Wall.** Retaining walls must be capped with a solid unit. Drainage voids and pinholes would obviously not be attractive in the final course. Manufacturers make cap units specific to their wall blocks and either make or recommend concrete adhesive that is applied with a caulking gun to secure cap blocks. An alternative to cap blocks is to adhere flat, natural stone, such as slate, on top of the final course. To place the cap course, clean off the top course and apply the adhesive. Lay the cap blocks next to one another and backfill with soil, not gravel. The backfill can then be planted with grass or other ground cover.

9 Continue assembling courses and backfilling until the wall reaches final height.

10 Lay the cap course using concrete adhesive. You can use special cap units or flat natural stone.

BUILDING STONE WALLS

In our hectic, high-tech lives in which computer keys are the closest many of us come to actually touching our work, stone masonry is refreshingly visceral. Sure, you'll do some layout measuring and run some guide strings, but stone is an irregular masonry unit that won't cooperate with precise measuring. Ultimately, the key to a sturdy and beautiful stone project lies in the judgments you make with your eyes and your hands. So enjoy the sun on your back, the sweat on your brow, and the dirt beneath your fingernails. In this chapter, you'll learn how to build stone walls (both dry-stacked and mortared), including retaining walls.

Choosing Stone

Although many types of stone are available throughout the country, only a few are suitable for building. Besides being accessible, suitable stones must satisfy certain requirements of strength, hardness, workability, and durability.

There are many ways to describe stone. It can be identified by the form in which it is used—rubble, ashlar, or flagstone. It can be identified by its type or mineral composition—granite, limestone, sandstone, slate, etc. And it can be described by the way in which it is obtained—fieldstone that is gathered from fields in its natural state and cut stone that is quarried with heavy equipment from large stone deposits. Stone can also be described in technical or scientific terms by its chemical composition or by its method of geological formation.

The familiar New England dry-stacked stone walls are made of fieldstone gathered from the fields by farmers as they clear the land for planting. The stones are most often a type of granite or sandstone, and they are laid in rubble form with little or no cutting.

Rubble Stone. Rubble stone is irregular in size and shape. Fieldstone collected in its natural form is a type of rubble, naturally rough and angular. Quarried rubble comes from the fragments of stone left over from the cutting and removal of large stone slabs. The difference between the two is that fieldstone rubble is weathered on all its surfaces, while quarried rubble has some freshly broken faces. Rubble stone can be laid in a number of different ways, depending on its size and shape and how you want it to look. Rubble can also be roughly squared with a brick hammer to make it fit together more easily. Rounded fieldstone or river stone is hard to work with because the curved surfaces make it difficult to stack the stone with the necessary stability.

Ashlar. Ashlar is stone that has been cut at the quarry to produce relatively smooth, flat bedding surfaces that stack easily. It is generally cut into small squares or rectangles and has sawn or dressed faces, but the face of ashlar may also be left slightly rough. The free-form look of a rubble wall is quite different from the formal appearance of an ashlar wall.

Common Types of Stone

The most common stones that satisfy the requirements of building construction are granite, limestone, sandstone, and slate. While many others, such as quartzite, bluestone, and serpentine, are available in some parts of the country, they are used less frequently.

Granite. Granite is an extremely hard, strong stone noted for its durability. Its color may be red, pink, brown, buff, green, gray, or black, depending on where it was quarried. The same hardness that makes granite so durable also makes sawing or cutting it very difficult. Granite that is cut and dressed is

expensive because the stone is so hard to work with, thus it is usually used only on luxury commercial projects. For outdoor garden and landscape applications, granite is usually available as quarried or fieldstone rubble.

Limestone. Limestone is relatively durable, easily worked, and widely available in many parts of the country. It's an attractive stone and is sometimes characterized by embedded shells and fossilized animals and plants. Although soft when first quarried, limestone becomes hard with age and exposure to the weather. Because it's much more porous than granite, limestone is not as durable in cold, rainy, or snowy areas where it is exposed to repeated cycles of freezing and thawing.

Limestone is most often cream or buff colored but may be reddish or yellowish or have a gray tint. When quarried, limestone contains ground water (commonly called quarry sap), which includes varying amounts of organic and chemical matter. Gray-

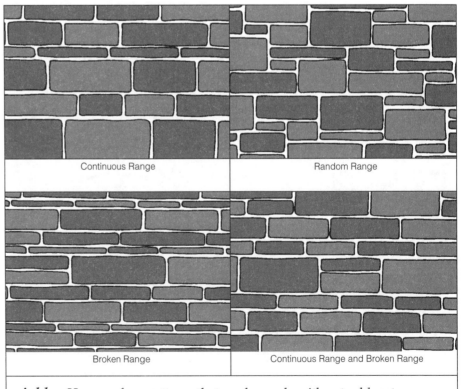

Ashlar. Here are four patterns that can be made with cut ashlar stone.

Stone is sold by the cubic yard at quarries and stone suppliers. Cut stone will naturally be more expensive than fieldstone or quarried rubble stone, because of the labor required to produce it. Since availability and cost can vary by region, it is best to visit suppliers before you plan your project—so you can base your design on materials that are readily available in your area and within your budget.

To estimate how many cubic yards of stone you will need, multiply the length times the height times the width of your wall in feet to get cubic feet, then divide by 27 to get cubic yards. If you are using ashlar stone, add about 10 percent to your order for breakage and waste. If you are using rubble stone, add at least 25 percent.

colored stone generally contains more natural moisture than buff-colored stone. As the quarry sap dries and stabilizes, the stone lightens in color and is said to "season." Buff stone will season in about 60 to 90 days, but gray stone may require seasoning for as long as six months. If unseasoned stone is placed in a wall, it may be very uneven in color for several months, or even as long as a year. There is no way to improve the appearance of the structure during the seasoning period. Left alone to weather, the stone eventually will attain its characteristic light neutral color.

Limestone is available as fieldstone and quarried rubble, as ashlar, and sometimes as flagstone. Because it is softer and more porous than granite, limestone is also easier to work with. It is easy to shape with simple tools.

Sandstone. You'll find sandstone in a variety of colors, ranging from buff, pink, and crimson to greenish brown, cream, and blue-gray. Light-colored sandstone is usually strong and durable. Reddish or brown sandstone is typically softer and more easily cut. Sandstone is available as fieldstone and quarried rubble, as ashlar, and as flagstone split into thin slabs for paving. Sandstone is easier to cut and work with than granite but more difficult than limestone.

Cutting & Shaping Stone

When you are laying stone in mortar, you often can hide slightly irregular shapes by burying them in the mortar joints. When you are dry-laying stones without mortar, the fit of the stones usually must be more precise both for aesthetics and stability. For both types of stonework though, you will often have to cut and shape individual stones to make them fit

better. Be sure to wear heavy leather gloves and safety goggles whenever you are cutting stone.

1 Scoring the Line. While granite is difficult to cut, limestone, sandstone, and slate are relatively easy to work with once you get the knack. First position the stone on solid ground for firm, even support. Do not lay the stone on concrete because the hard concrete surface may cause the stone to break in the wrong place. If you like, you can mark the cutting line with chalk, crayon, or pencil. Then use a pitching chisel to score the cut by positioning the flat edge of the chisel along the intended line and tapping lightly with the hammer.

2 Splitting the Stone. Often, the stone will break along the line before you have scored it all the way around. If not, strike one sharp blow to split the stone after scoring it. Remove any small bumps or protrusions with a point chisel, placing the point at the base of the bump and tapping with hammer.

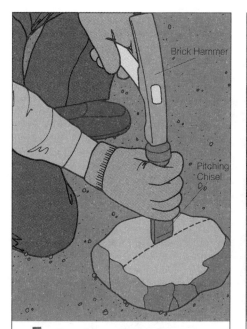

1 Lay the stone on flat ground for solid support. Use a pitching chisel and a hammer to lightly score a line where the stone is to be split.

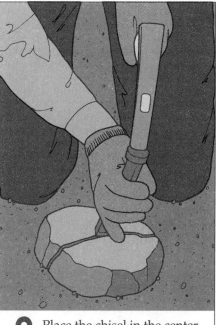

2 Place the chisel in the center of the scored line and strike it with a hammer to split the stone. Remove any bumps or protrusions with the chisel.

Building a Dry-Stacked Stone Wall

Dry-stacked stone walls are built without mortar. Friction, gravity, and the interlocking of the individual stones hold the wall together. Although the work is physically hard, the techniques involved are simple. A dry-stacked wall is a bit flexible; it can absorb some frost heave within the ground. As a result, a concrete footing is not usually required for dry-stack walls up to 3 feet high. You'll probably want to build no higher than 3 feet anyway, since it's tough to lift stones to that height. Also, most municipalities won't require a permit for a dry-stacked wall up to 4 feet high. But be sure to check with your local building department before building any wall. Even if no permit is required, there may be local zoning or planning regulations that will affect the construction and placement of your wall.

While construction techniques are straightforward, the stones may require some cutting and shaping to create good interlocking fits. Sandstone and limestone rubble usually are among the easiest to cut. If you are gathering rather than

buying fieldstone, look for angular not rounded shapes. Save the largest stones for the base course, the squarest ones for the ends and corners, and the flattest ones for the cap.

A dry-stacked stone wall consists of two "wythes," or vertical stacks.

This easily constructed slope gauge is designed to help ensure that the faces of your stone wall slope in at a rate of ½ inch per foot. Because this means that a wall face should slope a total of 1½ inches in 3 feet, it's simple to construct a 3-foot-long gauge from standard 1x4 lumber. (The actual dimensions of 1x4 lumber are ¾ by 1½ inches.)

The gauge has four parts; a slope board, a plumb board, a cross block, and a spacer block. Cut these parts from 1x4 stock to the lengths shown in the drawing. Assemble the gauge with 1¼-inch drywall screws. Predrill to prevent splitting the little spacer block; then attach it to the plumb board with a single screw. Fasten the slope board to the opposite end of the plumb board with one screw. Then screw the cross block to the spacer block and to the slope board.

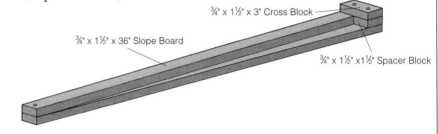

¾" x 1½" x 3" Cross Block

¾" x 1½" x 36" Slope Board

¾" x 1½" x 1½" Spacer Block

Space between the wythes is filled with small rubble, and the wythes are tied together every several feet with a bond stone that spans the entire thickness of the wall. Walls up to 3 feet high should have a base that's at least 2 feet thick. If you do build a higher wall, add at least 8 inches of thickness at the base for each foot of height. Each end and face of a dry-stacked wall must be "battered," or sloped inward ½ inch for every foot of height. The wall should sit in a 6-inch-deep trenched excavation. If necessary, 2 inches of sand can be placed in the bottom of the trench to improve drainage. If the ground slopes, dig the trench in a series of flat terraces.

1 Excavating the Trench. Set four wood stakes just beyond the ends of the proposed wall site and stretch mason's twine between the stakes to mark the sides of the wall. Excavate a trench 6 inches deep and as wide as you need for the base (usually 24 inches). If the soil contains a lot of clay or drains poorly for some other reason, you can improve drainage and stability by adding 2 inches of sand in the

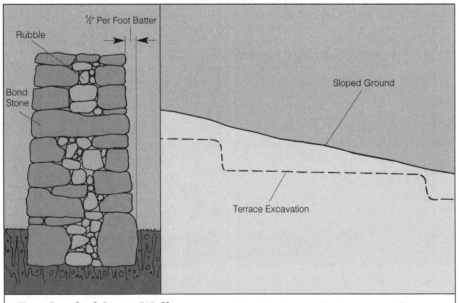

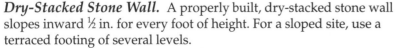

Dry-Stacked Stone Wall. A properly built, dry-stacked stone wall slopes inward ½ in. for every foot of height. For a sloped site, use a terraced footing of several levels.

bottom of the trench. Once the trench is dug, remove the stakes and twine.

2 Laying the First Course. Lay two wythes of large stones with their top surfaces tilted slightly down toward the center of the wall—so that they are lower in the middle than at the outside edges. Use your largest stones for the first course, not only to create a good base but also to avoid lifting and adjusting these heavy pieces higher up. The corners and ends of walls are particularly vulnerable to damage, so choose stones for these locations that fit well together to add stability. Position the stones so that their most attractive faces are exposed. Dig out under the stones or fill in spaces with soil to get the stones to sit flat without rocking. Fill the area in between the wythes with smaller stones. Pack the spaces between stones in this first course with soil to give the wall a stable base.

3 Laying the Second Course. Lay the next course, setting the stones on the face of the wall slightly in from the face of the stones below. Carefully select each stone for the best fit with its neighbors. The less you have to shim the stones with small pieces of rubble, the better. Trim and cut the stones to fit as necessary. If a stone rocks on a point or sharp corner, shape it to sit down more squarely. Check your work periodically with a 4-foot level to keep each course approximately level. Using a level to make sure the plumb board is plumb, hold the slope gauge against the wall to make sure that it tapers correctly from bottom to top. As before, set the large outside stones first, then fill in the middle with smaller stones.

4 Laying the Bond Stones. In each course, lay a bond stone

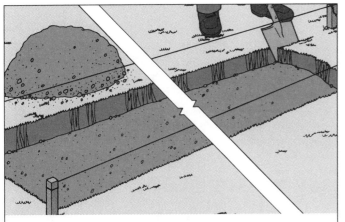

1 Lay out the trench with stakes and twine. Excavate 6 in. deep by 2 ft. wide. If drainage is a problem, allow for a 2-in. sand bed at the bottom of the excavation.

2 Use the largest stones for the first course. Place them firmly in the trench, but lean them inward to the wall's center. Fill the area between wythes with small stones.

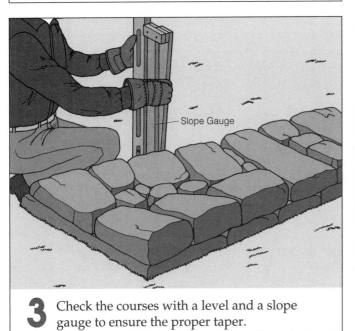

Slope Gauge

3 Check the courses with a level and a slope gauge to ensure the proper taper.

4 Lay a bond stone every 3 to 4 ft. to tie the wythes together.

that is the full width of the wall every 3 or 4 feet to tie the two halves of the wall together.

5 **Setting the Level String.** It's always a good idea to set a goal. Cut two stakes long enough to drive firmly into the ground while leaving enough to extend about 6 inches above your final wall height. Set the stakes so they are approximately centered across each end of the wall. Extend a mason's line between the stakes at the final wall height. Place a line level on the twine and adjust the twine until it is level. Throughout the building process, sight down the line to make sure your wall is running in a straight line. As you get to the last few courses

of stone, the level string will help you adjust your work so that the top of the wall will be level.

6 **Shimming as Needed.** If a stone does not sit firmly in place, break another stone into small pieces and use the pieces as shims. All the stones should be slightly inclined toward the center of the wall so that the weight leans in on itself.

7 **Filling the Wall.** After laying several courses of stone, fill in the small spaces along the face of the wall by driving in small stones with your hammer. This is called "chinking" and helps interlock the wall and tilt the stones inward.

8 **Laying Successive Courses.** The key to a stable wall is to avoid long uninterrupted vertical joints. To achieve this, always overlap the stones in successive courses. Stone masons call this the "one over two, two over one rule."

9 **Interlocking the Ends and Corners.** Interlock the ends and corners of the wall to provide stability. This is like dovetailing a carpentry joint, in which the two adjacent pieces are overlapped to form a strong connection. Use the stones that have the squarest sides and corners for these areas. Take your time and be patient with this part of the wall. If you can't find stones that fit well enough, try cutting

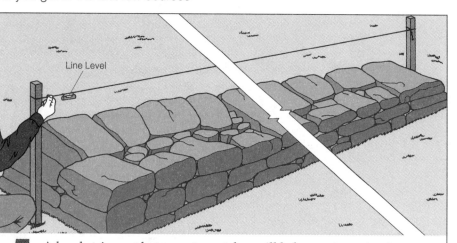

Line Level

5 A level string set between two stakes will help you to maintain a straight wall and keep the top course level. Set the stakes so they are approximately centered across each end of the wall.

6 Place small rock shims to set the stones snug and leaning in toward the center.

7 Chinking rocks into the gaps and holes will make a stronger structure.

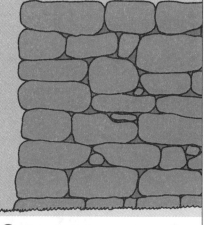

8 Use the "one over two, two over one rule" to avoid long vertical joints in the wall.

9 Overlap the stones with the squarest sides and corners at the wall's end.

and shaping some to form a strong, stable interlock.

10 Capping the Top of the Wall. Flat stones of roughly rectangular shape make the best caps. The top course should be as level as possible for the full length of the wall; in cold climates, many masons like to set the cap stones in mortar to protect the wall from moisture penetration and to prevent them from being knocked off. Mix the mortar in a wheelbarrow or mortar mixing box as described in "Mortar for Stone Walls," page 75. Trowel on a 1- to 2-inch-thick mortar bed, covering about 2 feet of the wall at a time. Fill in the joints between the cap stones with mortar, too, packing it firmly and using enough mortar so the surface joints are flat or slightly rounded and will not collect water.

10 Lay a rounded mortar cap on top of the final course to prevent water penetration and to bolster the strength of the wall.

Another attractive alternative is to use a cap of mortar on top of the last course to help tie the top of the wall together. You put the top course in a bed of mortar as described above and then add a mortar cap. Or you can use the mortar cap alone. In any case, make the mortar cap rounded to help shed water.

Stone Retaining Wall

A dry-stacked stone retaining wall relies on gravity, friction, and the interlock of the stones to resist the overturning motion of an earth embankment. Like the previous stone wall project, a dry-stacked retaining wall consists of two "wythes" or vertical stacks. A well-built dry-stacked retaining wall is superior to a mortared retaining wall because dry stacking leaves spaces for ground water to drain through. However, the stones may require considerable cutting and shaping to create the good interlocking fits that are key to a good dry-stacked wall. See "Cutting and Shaping Stone," on page 67. Easily workable stone like sandstone or limestone rubble will usually be best.

Dry-stacked stone retaining walls up to 3 feet high do not require a concrete footing. They may be laid directly onto the soil in a 6-inch-deep trench. For stability, the inside of the wall must tilt toward the embankment at least 2 inches for every foot of wall height. If you don't mind looking at a sloped outer face, you can simply tilt the entire wall back. If you prefer a plumb outer face, make the wall gradually thicker as you build up.

Terraced Walls. In addition to requiring a concrete footing, retaining walls of more than 3 feet high get tricky to build, and in many municipalities, you'll need a building permit if the wall is more than 4 feet tall. Often, a better alternative to a single high wall is to build two shorter walls stepped back against the slope. At the base, a 3-foot wall should be 18 inches thick.

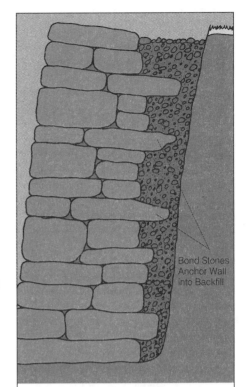

Stone Retaining Wall. A dry-stacked stone retaining wall will either tilt backward to the embankment or be thicker at the top. Backfill with gravel.

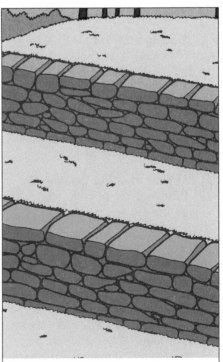

Terraced Walls. Rather than build a retaining wall more than 3 ft. high, build sections of shorter, terraced walls.

Building the Wall

1 Excavating the Trench. Cut the angle of the embankment back 30 to 45 degrees from plumb to give you room to place the stones and the gravel for drainage behind the stones. Loose or sandy soils tend to collapse, so cut the angle more sharply.

In soil that drains well, excavate a 6-inch-deep x 18-inch-wide trench along the length of the wall. Remove all grass, sod, roots, and large rocks. The first course of stones can be laid directly in the excavation.

In dense or clay soils or in areas that do not drain well, excavate 10 or 12 inches deep and add an 8- or 10-inch-deep gravel or crushed-stone drainage bed. Level the drainage bed with a rake and tamp the gravel or stone to compact it. Then lay down a layer of landscape fabric, which will allow moisture and air to penetrate but will prevent the sand from settling into the gravel. Overlap adjoining sections of fabric by 4 inches. Place a 2-inch bed of sand in the trench for leveling the stones.

2 Setting a String Line. A level base course is important to the stability of the wall. Drive wood stakes just beyond the ends of the excavation near the front face of the wall. Tie mason's twine between the stakes. Hang a line level on the twine and adjust the twine until it is level.

3 Laying the First Course of Stones. Starting at one end of the wall, lay the first course of stones. Carefully fit each one, seating it firmly in the soil or sand bed and following the string line for level. Use your largest stones for the first course, not only to create a good base but to avoid having to lift and adjust these heavy pieces at higher levels. Dig out under the stones or fill in spaces with soil, if necessary, to get the stones to sit flat without wobbling. Pack the spaces between stones in this first course with soil to give the wall a stable base.

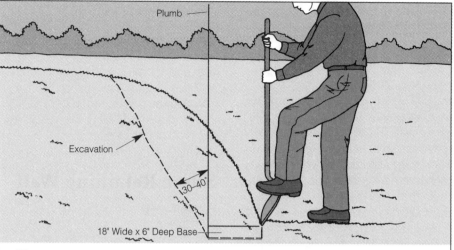

1 Excavate the embankment back 30 to 40 degrees from plumb. Dig deep enough for a gravel drainage base if needed.

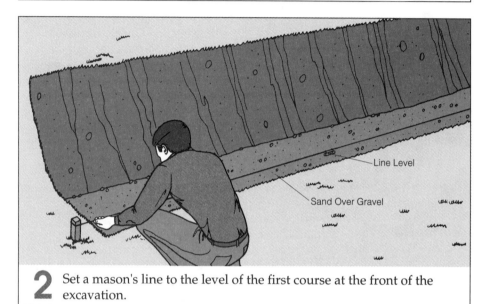

2 Set a mason's line to the level of the first course at the front of the excavation.

3 Lay the first course of stones. Either add or remove soil to ensure a level course. Fill any gaps between the stones with soil.

4 Setting Next Courses. Set the next few courses of stone on top of the first, keeping in mind that you want the inside of the wall to slant back at least 2 inches for every foot of height. As mentioned, the front of the wall can be plumb or it can follow the slope. Lay stones in successive courses so that they overlap the stones above and below. Avoid creating continuous, straight vertical joints. The overlapping pattern will produce a stronger wall, giving it the stability it needs to resist pressure from the soil. Install long stones that stick back into the backfill

about every 4 feet horizontally in each course. These are called bond stones or deadmen, and they help tie the wall into the hillside. Offset these bond stones in each course.

5 Adding Drainage Backfill. After the first few courses of stone are laid, begin adding gravel as drainage backfill behind the wall. Try to keep the gravel layer at least 6 inches thick.

6 Adding the Remaining Courses. Set the remaining courses of stone in the same manner. Remember to let each course of the

inside wythe jut an inch or so farther toward the embankment so that the inside face will slant about 2 inches per foot. When building up the wall, carefully select each stone for the best fit. Check the fit of each stone as you lay it. If a stone wobbles on a point or sharp corner, shape it to sit more securely. See "Cutting and Shaping Stone" on page 67. You also can use small pieces of stone as shims to make the stones fit more tightly together; although for the best-looking wall, you'll want to minimize shims. If you do use shims, insert them from the outside of the wall. All the stones should be slightly inclined toward the soil embankment so that the weight of the wall leans into the hill. While stones should fit snugly together in a retaining wall, don't worry about filling every little void between stones. You want to leave plenty of natural "weepholes" to allow groundwater to pass through. Check your work periodically with a mason's level to keep each course approximately level. Continue backfilling with gravel every two or three courses.

7 Capping the Top of the Wall. You have some design options here. One approach is to stop building 6 or 8 inches before you get to the top of the slope. Pack dirt between the top course of stones and then cover the top of the wall with soil to bring it up to the top

4 Place bond stones that jut into the backfill area every 4 ft. These will anchor the wall.

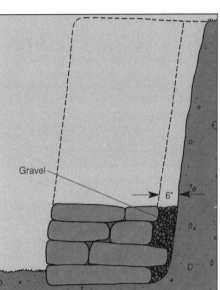

5 Add at least 6 in. of gravel backfill between the wall and the slope for drainage.

6 Place small stones as shims to lock the wall tightly together. Do not fill every gap in the wall; water must be allowed to pass through.

7 As a design option, lay 6 to 8 in. of dirt on the last course to bring the wall to top grade. Ground cover or grass can be planted in this soil.

grade. Then you can plant a ground cover on top of the wall. The plant's root network will help prevent erosion and help hold the top of the wall together. This approach looks great in a casual country garden.

Another approach is to leave the top of the wall exposed as you would for any freestanding stone wall. You can mortar the top course in place or cap the top course with mortar. See Step 10 "Capping the Top of the Wall" on page 71.

Mortared Stone Walls

A well-built dry-stacked wall will last for centuries, so why build a mortared wall? In most informal country or garden settings, there is no reason to use mortar, except, perhaps, for the cap; dry stacking is the way to go. Use mortar if you want a more formal look or if the wall is in a place where people are likely to walk on it, sit on it, or otherwise disturb the stones. Mortared walls require less maintenance; you won't have to worry about stones occasionally becoming dislodged.

Filling the spaces with mortar allows you to use more irregularly shaped stones. You still want to select stones carefully so you won't have an ugly wall with huge mortar joints, but individual stones needn't fit together quite so well as is necessary for a dry-stacked wall. As you would for any stone wall, save the largest stones for the base course, the squarest ones for the ends and corners, and the flattest ones for the cap. Rubble stone that is at least roughly squared on all sides will work best for mortared walls.

Mortar also helps prevent water from passing through a wall. This was more important when stone was commonly used for basement walls or solid stone house walls.

Like dry-stacked walls, most mortared stone walls are constructed with two vertical stacks, called wythes. Unlike dry-stacked walls that must be tapered as they rise, mortared walls are built straight up with plumb faces on both sides.

Construction is similar, but mortared walls are a lot more work than dry-stacked walls, not only because of the mortar but because they require

a steel-reinforced concrete footing below the frost line. This footing is required because mortar makes the wall into a stiff monolith that will crack if subjected to frost heave. A dry-stacked wall can absorb some frost heave movement with no damage.

Designing the Footing

Design and build a steel-reinforced footing as described in "Concrete Footings," page 10. As a general rule, make the footing thickness equal to the wall width, and twice as wide as the wall width. Check with your local building department for requirements about footings in your area. If the footings must be set very deep, it may be more economical to build a concrete wall to within a few inches of grade rather than building several courses of stone below ground level.

Stepped Footing. If your wall travels down a hill, build your footings as a series of level steps. Stepped footings are also described in "Concrete Footings," page 10. For flatter slopes, build a footing that is deep enough so that its bottom is below the frost line and its top is level for the full length of the wall.

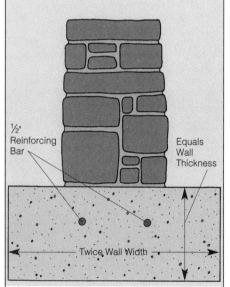

½"
Reinforcing Bar

Equals Wall Thickness

Twice Wall Width

Designing the Footing. Overlap the stones with the squarest sides and corners at the wall's end.

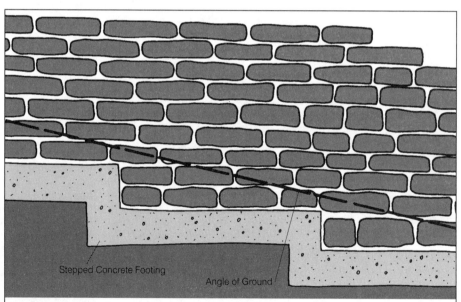

Stepped Concrete Footing

Angle of Ground

Stepped Footing. A stepped concrete footing creates level surfaces for the wall construction.

Mortar for Stone Walls

Masonry mortar is made with the same types of portland cements typically used in concrete. See "Mortar," page 24. The most common is a Type I general-purpose cement. Mortar for stone walls should be a mixture of one part lime, two parts portland cement, and nine parts sand. The lime should be a hydrated mason's lime; the sand should be a well-graded masonry sand with a range of fine to coarse grains. Some manufacturers produce factory-blended masonry cements that are combinations of either portland cement and lime or portland cement and other natural or chemical agents. For small projects, masonry cements are more convenient because all that is required is the addition of sand and water. Naturally, you'll pay more for this convenience. Mix one part of the masonry cement with three parts sand.

Mortar must be consistent from batch to batch or the color and texture will vary. Mortar usually is mixed by volume proportions using a container of convenient size for consistent proportioning. Always use a container for measuring ingredients so that the proportional volume of materials is the same each time. A 1 or 2 gallon plastic bucket is a good choice and is not too heavy when full. Don't pack the materials in the bucket and don't mix more than you can use in about three hours; mortar usually sets up in three to four hours. Mortar is useless once it hardens.

If your materials cannot be stored close to where you'll be working, mix your mortar in a wheelbarrow so you can move it easily. If you are using a mortar box, make sure it's level so water won't collect in one end or a corner.

Mixing Mortar. First, measure all the dry ingredients and mix them thoroughly with a mason's hoe. Blending will go more easily if you put half the sand in first, then the cement and lime mixture, and then add the rest of the sand. Alternately, pull and push the materials back and

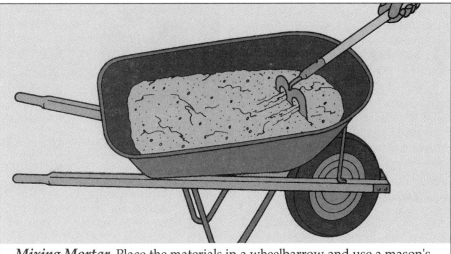

Mixing Mortar. Place the materials in a wheelbarrow and use a mason's hoe to push and pull the mortar ingredients together.

forth until the color is even. Then push the mix to one end of the mortar box or wheelbarrow, or make a hole in the middle, and pour 2 gallons of water in the hole or the empty end of the mixing box to start. Measure the water. Don't use a garden hose because it's too easy to get too much water. Using a chopping motion with the hoe, mix the dry ingredients into the water, pushing and pulling the mix back and forth until the consistency is uniform.

The amount of moisture in the sand will influence how much water is needed in a mortar mix to get the right consistency. If you buy bags of sand for small projects, it will be dry. If you buy sand in bulk by the ton for larger projects, it will be damp or wet. You should keep your sand pile covered so that the moisture content will not change drastically in wet or dry weather.

Masonry mortar for brick and block work should be the consistency of soft mud. But because stone is so heavy, a relatively stiff mix is better here, even though it is a little more difficult to work with. Mortar for stone uses more sand than normal. If the mix is still too dry after you add the initial 2 gallons of water, add more water in small quantities until the consistency is right. To check for proper consistency, make a series of sharp ridges in the mortar with

the hoe or trowel. If the ridges appear dry and crumbly, more water is needed. Ridges that stay sharp without slumping indicate the right consistency. If you add too much water, add proportional amounts of cement, lime, and sand to bring the mortar back to the proper consistency.

Within the first two hours after mixing, mortar can be retempered once with a little water to replace evaporated moisture and restore proper consistency. In hot, dry, or windy weather, the time limits on retempering may be shorter. Do not retemper more than once; mortar that has begun to harden must be discarded because it will not develop a good bond with the stone.

Building a Mortared Stone Wall

1 Snapping a Chalk Line. After the footing has cured for a few days, brush any dirt and debris from the surface. Measure and mark the location of the outside face of the wall, being careful to center the masonry in the middle of the footing. Square your corners and snap a chalk line along the length of the footing. Then snap another line to define the back of the wall. If your footing will form one or more corners, use the 3-4-5 triangle method described in "Locating and

Excavating" page 10, to make sure the corners are square.

2 Laying Stone in a Test Run.
First lay the stone on the footing in a test course without mortar, laying the outside row of stones along the chalk line. Carefully select and fit the stones, turning them back and forth to get a secure, stable fit. Lay larger stones along the two outside faces of the wall; fill in the middle with smaller stones.

Mortared stone walls must have bond stones that extend through the full thickness of the wall. These will help hold the front and back wythes together. Space the bond stones every 3 feet or so horizontally and vertically. When you build the wall, stagger the bond stone positions in successive courses rather than putting the bond stones directly above each other.

3 Spreading Mortar.
Mix a batch of mortar as described in "Mortar for Stone Walls" on page 75, using one part lime, two parts portland cement, and nine parts sand or simply use one part masonry cement to three parts sand.

After laying out the first course in a test run, remove a few stones at one end of the wall and begin to spread the mortar in a bed joint about 2 inches thick. Keep the mortar about ½ inch inside your guidelines, because it will spread when you lay the stone. This first course is very important—you want to lay enough mortar so that the bed joint doesn't develop voids when you lay the stones on it. Spread only enough mortar at one time to keep just ahead of your stone laying.

4 Laying Stone.
Brush or wash off any dirt or sand on the stones that would prevent the mortar from sticking. Start at one end of the wall or at a corner; lay the corner or end stone first, pressing it firmly down into the mortar and tapping it lightly with the trowel handle if necessary. To help keep the front

of the wall straight, lay each outside face stone before you lay the stone behind it. To keep the stones clean as you work, have a bucket of water and a sponge handy to immediately wipe off spilled mortar.

5 Filling in between Outside Stones.
Fill in the center of the wall with smaller, odd-size rubble stones. Add mortar on top of the fill stones as needed to make the course level. Use the trowel to throw mortar in between these stones and the larger ones, forming the outside faces of the wall. Finish the entire first course before beginning the second course.

6 Raking the Mortar Joints.
As you lay the wall, rake the mortar joints to accent the shape

1 Snap chalk lines to mark the front and back of the wall on the footing.

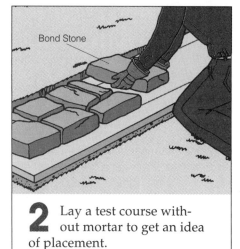

Bond Stone

2 Lay a test course without mortar to get an idea of placement.

3 Remove some stones at the end and lay 2 in. of mortar, ½ in. from the chalk lines.

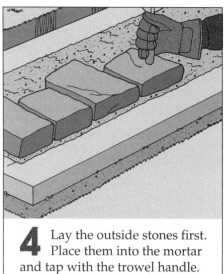

4 Lay the outside stones first. Place them into the mortar and tap with the trowel handle.

5 Fill in the middle of the outside stones with small rubble stones. Throw mortar between all the stones.

of the stones. If the stones have sharp edges, rake the joints out about ½ inch. If the edges are slightly rounded or broken, rake the joints out about 1 inch. Use the rounded end of a broom handle or a ⅜-inch round-headed bolt to do the raking. Remove excess mortar with a whisk broom. If you prefer the look of a joint that is flush with the face of the stones, just use the whisk broom without raking.

7 Tooling the Mortar Joints.
After the mortar begins to cure, you need to tool the surfaces of the joints to compress the mortar. It is

important that the joints be tooled to a consistent moisture content, so they don't appear light in some areas and dark in others. The joints are ready for tooling when the mortar is "thumbprint" hard, meaning the you can press your thumb against the mortar and leave a print impression without mortar sticking to your thumb. Don't wait until you have finished a large section of wall before you tool the joints —check the mortar frequently, and tool the joints a few at a time. As you tool the joints, small pieces of mortar called "tailings" will squeeze out—remove them with a soft-bristled brush.

8 Setting the Level Line.
Set wood stakes at the front corners of the wall and stretch mason's twine between them. Tie the line about 3 or 4 inches above the top of the next course. This will help you keep the courses of stone approximately level and the wall straight.

9 Building the Leads.
After setting the line, build leading sections, or "leads," at the ends or corners. Masonry walls are always laid from the outside ends or corners toward the middle; the leads help establish the correct spacing and coursing heights for the rest of the wall. Select your squarest, most regular stones for the leads. Before the mortar sets, use a 4-foot level to check that your leads are plumb on the ends and both faces.

10 Laying the Middle Courses.
Test fit several stones at a time. Follow the "one over two, two over one rule" that was described for dry-stacked walls. That is, try to make every stone cover a joint between two stones below so that you don't create continuous vertical joints. After test fitting, remove the stones, apply mortar, and fit the stones back into place to fill in the middle courses of the wall. When fitting stones against one another, spread mortar only on the stone already in place. Be generous with

6 Rake the joints with a broom handle or bolt. Use a whisk broom to remove excess mortar from the raked joints.

7 When the mortar is thumbprint hard, use a jointing tool to smooth and compress the joints.

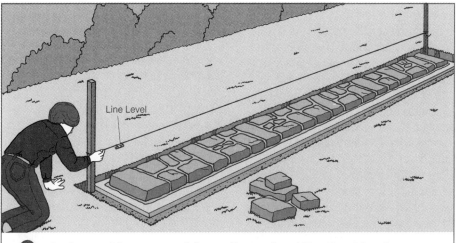

8 At the outside corners of the wall, set a level line 3 to 4 in. above the top of the course being laid. This will keep the wall straight and level.

9 Select the squarest stones to build the leads at the corners and ends of the wall.

10 After test fitting, apply mortar and lay stones in courses to fill between the leads.

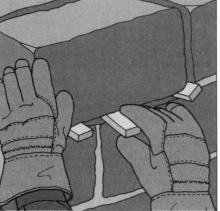

11 Insert wood wedges to support stones until the mortar sets.

12 Lay bond stones in the courses at a distance of about every 3 ft.

the amount and work it in so you don't have voids. Move the mason's twine up as you work to keep the courses roughly level. After setting each stone, tap it lightly with the trowel handle to eliminate air bub-bles in the mortar. Be careful not to get mortar on the face of the stones. If you do, remove it with a wet sponge before it dries. Don't let mortar droppings build up at the base of the wall—remove them as you go. When you finish each course, fill in between the wythes with small rubble stones.

11 **Inserting Wedges.** Because they are so heavy, it is sometimes necessary to temporarily support large stones with wood wedges to keep the mortar from squeezing out of the joints. Wet the wedges before you use them so they won't wick water out of the mortar. Once the mortar has set, remove the wedges and fill the holes with more mortar.

12 **Laying the Bond Stones.** Remember to lay bond stones across both wythes about every 3 feet horizontally. Remember to stagger the bond stones so the joints do not all align vertically. Don't lay more than two courses of stone in a day—the mortar needs time to set up enough to support the weight.

13 Place flat cap stones on a thick bed of mortar on the top of the wall. Compress the joints with a jointing tool.

13 **Capping the Wall.** The top of a masonry wall requires special care and attention because it must protect the rest of the wall from rain and snow. The stones in the top course should be flat or slightly rounded on the top. Ideally, you want flat stones that are wide enough to span the full thickness of the wall. Even for a rubble wall, you may want to purchase cut stones for the cap course. Place a thick bed of mortar and set the cap stones on top of the wall. Make sure the joints between stones are completely filled with mortar; tool them to compress the surface of the mortar. Don't rake out the top joints as you did with those on the

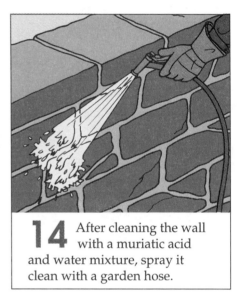

14 After cleaning the wall with a muriatic acid and water mixture, spray it clean with a garden hose.

sides of the wall or they will collect water. If you like, you can top the wall with a layer of mortar. Make the mortar cap rounded to help shed water.

14 **Cleaning the Wall.** After the wall has set for about a week, you can clean excess mortar off the face of the stones using a solution of 10 parts water to 1 part muriatic acid. Mix the solution in a plastic, not a metal, bucket. Pour the water in first, then add the acid to it. Wet the wall with a garden hose, apply the cleaning solution, then immediately rinse the wall again with the hose to stop the etching action of the acid. Be sure to wear rubber gloves and goggles when working with acid.

Aggregate Crushed stone, gravel, or other material added to cement to make concrete or mortar. Gravel and crushed stone are considered course aggregate; sand is considered fine aggregate.

Bat A brick that is cut in half lengthwise.

Broom Finish The texture created when a concrete surface is stroked with a stiff broom while the concrete is still curing.

Building Bricks These bricks, also called common bricks, are rough in appearance but structurally sound. Building bricks have chips, cracks, and slight deformations.

Buttering Placing mortar on a masonry unit using a trowel.

Collar Joint The vertical joint between wythes.

Concave Joint A masonry joint that is recessed and formed in mortar with a curved steel jointing tool.

Concrete Fresh concrete is a semifluid mixture of portland cement, sand, gravel or crushed stone, and water.

Concrete Block A masonry unit which consists of an outside shell with a hollow center that is divided by two or three vertical webs. The ends of the unit may have flanges that accept mortar and join with adjacent blocks, or they may have smooth ends for corners and the ends of walls.

Construction Joints A joint that is installed wherever a concrete pour is interrupted for more than 30 minutes or stopped at the end of the day.

Control Joints Special joints, also called contraction joints, which are tooled into the surface and make concrete crack in straight lines at planned locations.

Darby A long tool used for smoothing the surface of a concrete slab.

Edging Joints The rounded edges of a pour that are resistant to cracking.

Face Brick A type of brick used when consistency in appearance is required. A batch of face brick will be quite uniform in color, size, texture, and face structure.

Fire Brick A brick made of a special clay and baked at an extremely high temperature to make the unit resistant to heat.

Flashing Masonry flashing can be made of metal, rubberized asphalt sheet membranes, or other materials. It is used to control moisture in masonry walls either by keeping the top of a wall dry or by collecting water inside a wall so that it can be drained out through weep holes.

Floating The process of smoothing the surface of a pour with a float made of steel, aluminum, magnesium, or wood. This action drives large aggregate below the surface.

Footing Concrete footings are used to support garden walls of brick, block, or stone.

Formwork The forms, or molds, that contain and shape wet concrete. Forms are usually built from lumber; plywood is used for curved sections.

Frost Heave Shifting or upheaval of the ground resulting from alternate freezing and thawing of water in the soil.

Frost Line The maximum depth to which soil freezes in the winter. The local building department can provide information on the frost line depth in your area.

Header The brick position in a wall in which the brick is rotated 90 degrees from the stretcher position so that the ending is facing out.

Hydration The process of cement particles chemically reacting with water. When this happens the concrete hardens into a durable material.

Isolation Joints Strips in formwork that separate new concrete from existing adjacent construction and other concrete slabs that might expand and contract differently or experience different soil settlement or other movement.

Mortar A mixture of cementitious materials, fine aggregate, and water. Mortar is used to bond bricks or blocks.

Nominal Dimensions The measured dimensions of a masonry unit plus one mortar joint.

Portland Cement A mixture of burned lime, iron, silica, and alumina. This mixture is put through a kiln and then ground into a fine powder and packaged for sale. The cement is the same color as the gray limestone quarried near Portland, England.

Prepackaged Concrete Mix A mix that combines cement, sand, and gravel in the correct proportions and requires only the addition of water to create fresh concrete.

Ready-Mix Concrete Wet concrete that is transported from a concrete supplier. The concrete is ready to pour.

Rebar Reinforcing bar (called rebar for short) is used for concrete that will carry a heavy load, such as footings, foundation walls, columns, and pilasters.

Reinforcing Mesh Steel wires woven or welded into a grid of 6- or 10-inch squares. The mesh is primarily used in flatwork, such as sidewalks, patios, and driveways.

Rowlock A brick laid on its face edge so that the end is visible in the wall.

Sailor A brick standing upright with the face positioned out.

Screeding Using a straight 2x4 moved from one end of a concrete pour to the other to strike off excess concrete.

Segregation A condition that results when the concrete is overworked—such as when trying to remove air bubbles—and the water separates and rises to the top.

Soap A brick that is halved in width.

Soldier A brick standing upright, edge facing out.

Split A brick that is halved in height.

Stretcher A brick that is laid lengthwise in the course.

Troweling Finishing the concrete after it has been screeded. This finishing step is for interior concrete applications and concrete without air-entrainment.

Wall Coping The final course of material or masonry units on a brick wall. Coping a brick wall ties the masonry units together and helps retard water penetration.

Weep Hole A hole in a retaining wall that allows water to seep through and thus relieve pressure against the wall.

Wythe The vertical section of a wall that is equal to the width of the masonry unit.